SECOND EDITION

ALPINE FLOWER FINDER

The Key to
Rocky Mountain Wildflowers
Found Above Treeline

JANET L. WINGATE & LORAINE YEATTS

Johnson Books
BOULDER

Published by Johnson Books, a division of Johnson Publishing Company,
1880 South 57th Court, Boulder, Colorado 80301.
Visit our website at www.JohnsonBooks.com. E-mail: books@jpcolorado.com

Cover design by Debra B. Topping
Cover photo, *Sedum rhodanthum*, by Loraine Yeatts
9 8 7 6 5 4 3 2 1

Library of Congress Cataloging-in-Publication Data
Wingate, Janet L.
   Alpine flower finder: the key to Rocky Mountain wildflowers found
above timberline/Janet L. Wingate and Loraine Yeatts.—2nd ed.

     p. cm.
   ISBN 1-55566-289-7
   1. Wild flowers—Rocky Mountain Region—Identification. 2. Mountain
plants—Rocky Mountains Region—Identification. 3. Wildflowers—Rocky
Mountains Region—Pictorial works. 4. Mountain plants—Rocky Mountain
Region—Pictorial works. I. Yeatts, Loraine. II. Title.
   QK139.W44 2003
   582.13'0978—dc21   2003000601

♻ Printed on recycled paper with soy ink.

This book includes over 350 species of wildflowers found in six U.S. Rocky Mountain states, ID, MT, WY, UT, CO, NM. Although not comprehensive it contains most common and showy alpine flowers. Unlike picture books, which are not necessarily definitive and require considerable page shuffling, this guide offers a quick, sure-fire method of on-site plant identification.

Features:
- ► Quick advice to beginners on how to use this key
- ► Minimal use of technical terminology
- ► Short illustrated glossary of all terms needed to use book
- ► Key (logical, user friendly, stepwise classification scheme) to plant families
- ► Key to plant species scientific and common names
- ► Line drawings of most species for instant gratification
- ► Color, habitat, and range information for each plant
- ► Index to scientific and common plant names

Careful examination of the following pages will start you in the right direction and enable you to rapidly step through the key.

white to pink

FF
Sc
R
T

Alpine Dusty Maiden
Chaenactis alpina

Find some **typical flowers** and **leaves** of the plant you want to identify, then turn to the key on page 1, make the first choice, second choice, etc. and proceed from there.

Example

►If plant has characteristic A
AND characteristic

Choice 1	Choice 2	►A1———————go to page x
		►A2———————go to page xx
		►A3———————go to page xxx

►If plant has characteristic B
AND characteristic

Choice 2	►B1———————go to page z
	►B2———————go to page zz

Typical flowers and **leaves** are found on average plants of the population, NOT giants, runts or misfits. Plants are inherently variable in all characters, which can make identification tricky.

► Study the following three pages for useful information and definition of terms. Refer to the glossary often to learn unfamiliar terms. Practice speed keying.
   PRACTICE PRODUCES PROFICIENCY
► Pick and take apart a flower if its parts are used in the key (only if there are plenty).
► A 10x hand lens will help you see small parts and the elegance of minature flowers.
► A 1cm scale line by the illustration indicates plant size. ┌─────┐
► Closely related plants are in **families** that appear in alphabetical order by their scientific family names. Scientific names comprised of **genus** and **species** names follow regional common names in the text.
► Similar plants and the characters by which they differ are occasionally mentioned after the illustrated plant.
► Color plants you have identified with colored pencils. HAVE FUN!

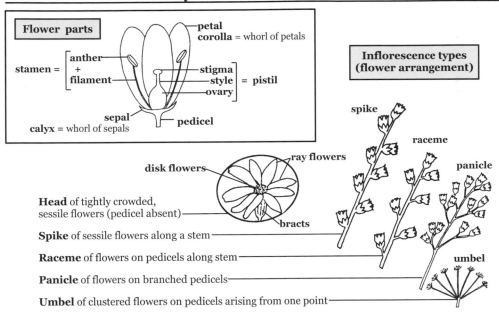

Flower parts

petal
corolla = whorl of petals

stamen = [anther + filament]

stigma
style
ovary
= pistil

sepal
pedicel
calyx = whorl of sepals

Inflorescence types (flower arrangement)

spike

raceme

panicle

umbel

ray flowers

disk flowers

bracts

Head of tightly crowded, sessile flowers (pedicel absent)

Spike of sessile flowers along a stem

Raceme of flowers on pedicels along stem

Panicle of flowers on branched pedicels

Umbel of clustered flowers on pedicels arising from one point

Glossary – terms that describe flowers

Regular flowers
have all petals alike.

Irregular flowers
have petals of different
shapes and sizes.

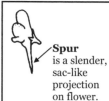

Spur
is a slender,
sac-like
projection
on flower.

Bract
is a leaf-like
appendage at
base of flower or
on stem below inflorescence.

Superior ovary
is above petals
and sepals.

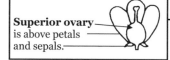

Inferior ovary
is below
petals and
sepals.

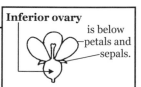

Separate petals
are free to the base and can
be removed one at a time.

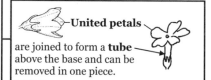

United petals
are joined to form a **tube**
above the base and can be
removed in one piece.

Fruit
is a mature ripe
ovary

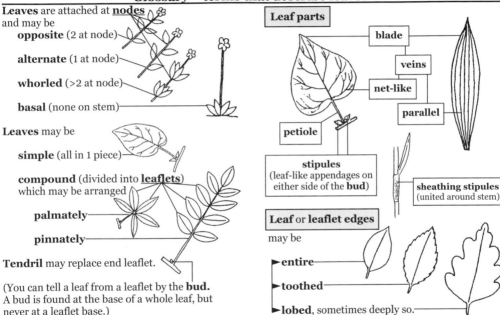

Leaves are attached at <u>**nodes**</u>
and may be

    opposite (2 at node)

    alternate (1 at node)

    whorled (>2 at node)

    basal (none on stem)

Leaves may be

    simple (all in 1 piece)

    compound (divided into **leaflets**)
    which may be arranged

        palmately

        pinnately

Tendril may replace end leaflet.

(You can tell a leaf from a leaflet by the **bud.**
A bud is found at the base of a whole leaf, but
never at a leaflet base.)

Leaf parts

blade

veins

net-like

parallel

petiole

stipules
(leaf-like appendages on
either side of the **bud**)

sheathing stipules
(united around stem)

Leaf or **leaflet edges**

may be

►**entire**

►**toothed**

►**lobed**, sometimes deeply so.

Habitat

R Rock outcrop – Barren environment with little or no soil, high solar intensity, extreme wind and temperature fluctuations, little moisture available.

T Talus – Accumulation of gravity sorted large to small rocks on unstable slopes.

FF Fellfield – Gentle slope or windswept ridgetop with little snow cover and 30-50% bare rock interspersed with mat plants, mosses and lichens.

Sc Scree – Accumulations of unsorted small rocks.

G Gravel – Uniform scree.

M Meadow – More than 50% plant cover on flat to gentle slope composed of mineral soil of alluvial or fellfield evolution.

K Krummholz – Stunted trees and shrubs near treeline.

Sn Snowbed – Area below melting snow.

St Streambank, lake or pond shore.

U Unstable or disturbed area.

W Wet or moist most of the season.

D Dry most of the season after snow has melted.

Range

Area covered by this book includes parts of
Idaho (**ID**)
Montana (**MT**)
Wyoming (**WY**)
Utah (**UT**)
Colorado (**CO**)
New Mexico (**NM**)
Dots on map indicate states in which a plant grows above treeline. Plant species may also occur in states or areas not covered by this book. State acronyms are sometimes qualified by: **n** (north), **s** (south), **e** (east), **w** (west), **c** (central).

Abbreviations

>	greater than	**mm**	millimeter
≥	greater than or equal to	**cm**	centimeter
<	less than	**m**	meter
≤	less than or equal to	**in**	inch
±	approximately or somewhat	**ft**	feet
		p	page

Begin Here   Choose the group that BEST fits your plant, and go from there.

►**Mat Plants** next page
  Plant forms hard mat that you can't poke your finger through.
►**Shrubs** page 4
  Plant has woody stems, obviously shrubby (look carefully).
►**No Petals** page 5
  Flower lacks petals.
►**Sunflower Family** page 22
  "Flower" is daisy-like, button-like, thistle-like or furry pussytoe-like.
  This is actually a head of many tiny flowers, see diagrams on pages v, 22
►**Tiny Flowers** page 6
  Individual flower tiny enough to entirely fit into 6mm diameter circle ◯
►**Large Flowers** (too large for circle) and they are
  ►**regular with separate petals** page 10
    Flowers are radially symmetric and each petal is separate from the next.
  ►**regular with united petals** page 14
    Flowers are radially symmetric and petal edges are partially united to
    each other to form a tube topped by lobes. To determine petal number
    count corolla lobes.
  ►**irregular** page 17
    Flower is bilaterally symmetric. Example: sweet pea, pansy, snapdragon.

2 **Key to Mat Plants** Plant forms hard mat that you can't poke your finger through.

►**Flowers blue, pink or purplish** ————————————— next page
►**Flowers yellow or yellowish**, AND
  ►in daisy-like heads ———————————————**Stemless Goldenweed** p37
  ►inconspicuous; mat very hard and flat ——————————**Alpine Nailwort** p58
  ►with four petals; flowers several, clustered ——————**Mustard Family** p48
  ►with five petals; stamens numerous; leaves compound————**Potentilla** p106
  ►with six petals; leaves with underside densely woolly hairy—**Buckwheat Family** p87

►**Flowers white**, AND
  ►one per stem, AND
    ►with lobes opened flat, perpendicular to tube ————————**Phlox** p85
    ►large with eight petals ————————————————**Alpine Dryad** p103
    ►with reddish stamens; rare ————————————————**Kelseya** 103
    ►NOT as above ————————————————**Alpine Sandwort** p60
  ►more than one per stem, AND
    ►with spotted petals ————————————————**Dotted Saxifrage** p113
    ►with yellow or red center (eye) ——————————————**Rockjasmine** p93
    ►in a ball; leaves with underside densely woolly hairy ——**Buckwheat Family** p87
    ►in a congested spike with many protruding stamens ————**Rockmat** p102
    ►with six stamens ————————————————**Mustard Family** p48

►**Flowers sky to pale blue, or sometimes white with yellow center (eye);** plant silvery hairy————————**Alpine Forget-me-not** p46

►**Flowers pink to purplish or bluish;** leaves
  ► compound with
    ►three leaflets; flowers large————————————————**Dwarf Clover** p66
    ►more than three leaflets, spine-tipped; flowers tiny, pea type————————————————**Mat Milkvetch** p71
  ► simple; flowers
    ►several per stem; leaves woolly hairy on underside————**Buckwheat Family** p87
    ►one per stem, with
      ►lobes opened flat, perpendicular to narrow tube————————————————————————**Phlox** p85
      ►squarish-tipped petals————————**Rocky Mountain Douglasia** p93
      ►united reddish sepals AND very narrow leaves————————**Moss Campion** p57
      ►pink stamens and separate petals; rare————————————**Kelseya** p103
      ►a two horned pistil ; ID, MT, WY————————————**Purple Saxifrage** p111

4 Key to Shrubs

►Leaves simple AND entire; flowers
  ►yellow; stems
    white————————————————————————**Whitestem Goldenweed** p28
    NOT white———————————————————————**Shrubby Goldenweed** p38
  ►pink or whitish, with petals
    ►united, urn- or bell-shaped ————— **Heath Family** p63
    ►separate; restricted range in ID——————————————**Kelseya** p103
  ►white to pinkish furry catkins,
    without petals——————————————————————**Willow Family** p109

►Leaves simple, lobed AND/OR toothed; leaves

  ►palmately lobed like this ; stems often spiny————**Currant Family** p77

  ►finely toothed; plants over 30cm (1ft) tall;
    flowers in fuzzy, flat-topped cluster———————————**Pink Spiraea** p102

►Leaves compound; plant
  ►spiny————————————————————————————**Raspberry** p104
  ►NOT spiny————————————————————————**Shrubby Potentilla** p105

► **Leaves alternate AND simple;** stems
  ► woody; flowers
    ► white, furry catkins ——————————————**Willow Family** p109
    ► yellow, in heads ——————————————**Whitestem Goldenweed** p28

  ► NOT woody OR if woody then white hairy;
    flowers (or heads)
    ► button-like, pussytoe-like or thistle-like
      (disk flowers group)——————————————**Sunflower Family** p22

    ► in a spike ——————————————**Wyoming Kittentails** p117

► **Leaves opposite AND simple** ——————————————**Pink Family** p57

► **Leaves compound;** leaflets number
  ► three ——————————————**Alpine Meadowrue** p99

  ► more than three, AND
    ► appear whorled, very numerous ——————————————**Gordon's Ivesia** p108

    ► are deeply lobed and fern-like but NOT whorled ——————————————**Sage** p26

6   Key to Tiny Flowers

Use this key if the entire flower is small
enough to fit into this 6mm diameter circle. ◯
If the plant forms a hard mat, see page 2.

►**Stem leaves alternate AND simple AND entire**————————next page
►**Stem leaves alternate AND simple AND
 toothed or shallowly lobed**————————————————page 8
►**Stem leaves opposite OR whorled**————————————page 8
►**Stem leaves absent OR sometimes one OR bract-like**——page 9
►**Stem leaves alternate AND compound or deeply lobed;**
 flowers
  ►pink or white and look like this or this ; leaves
    ►palmately divided————————————————**Woodland Star** p111
    ►pinnately divided and spine-tipped; flowers pea type————**Mat Milkvetch** p71
  ►in umbels, white, yellow or brownish purple————————**Parsley Family** p18
  ►in racemes; petals four, white or yellow————————**Mustard Family** p48
  ►in heads; inflorescence
    ►spike-like raceme or panicle with yellowish or reddish flowers————**Sage** p26
    ►flat-topped with white or pink-tinged flowers————————**Yarrow** p40
  ►in yellowish green ball————————————————**Gordon's Ivesia** p108
  ►yellowish; leaflets three and three-toothed like this ————**Sibbaldia** p106
  ►yellow, shiny with numerous stamens————————**Drab Buttercup** p98

flowers (continued)

►blue OR white with eye and shaped like this ————————————**Borage Family** p46

►blue and shaped like a funnel ————————————————**Bellflower Family** p56

►minute and reddish, greenish, OR whitish;
  sheathing stipules————————————————————————**Sorrel** p87

►pinkish and shaped like an urn or bell ————————————**Heath Family** p63

►yellowish brown in button-like umbels————————**American Thoroughwort** p18
►hidden in fur-tipped white, pink, or brownish
  clustered heads————————————————————————**Pussytoes** p29

►in white furry catkins ; stems woody————————————**Willow Family** p109

►white OR pinkish in a cottonball raceme; sheathing stipules ————————**Bistort** p88
►white, pink OR yellow with four petals————————————**Mustard Family** p48
►white, pink OR reddish with six petals————————————**Lily Family** p79
►white with stamens protruding from tight spike; mat plant————————**Rockmat** p102

►**Stem leaves alternate, toothed or shallowly lobed;** flowers
  ►white; leaves
    ►shaped like this 〈/ or this 〔〕————————————————**Saxifrage Family** p111
    ►toothed like this————————————————**Mustard Family** p48
  ►crimson in flat-topped cluster; petals pointed; leaves fleshy————**Kingscrown** p62
  ►pink, and
    ►in fuzzy spikes; leaves finely toothed like this ▱————**Kittentails** p117

    ►urn-shaped 〇 〇————————————————————————**Heath Family** p63
  ►yellow; leaves deeply lobed————————————————————**Buttercup Family** p95
  ►blue————————————————————————————**Alpine Speedwell** p123
►**Stem leaves opposite;** flowers
  ►pink with four petals————————————————————————**Willowherb** p82
  ►white and urn-shaped; leaves all simple————————**White Mountain Heather** p63
  ►blue or purple————————————————————————**Figwort Family** p117
  ►pure white OR yellowish green stars; leaves all simple————————**Pink Family** p57
  ►white, greenish or pinkish; some leaves usually
    deeply lobed or compound; stamens three————————**Valerian Family** p127

►**Stem leaves whorled;** leaves densely
  woolly hairy on undersurface ——————————————— **Buckwheat Family** p87

tiny flowers (from page 6)

▶**Leaves entire OR shallowly lobed or toothed, AND**
  ▶woolly hairy on undersurface————————————**Buckwheat Family** p87
  ▶NOT woolly hairy on undersurface; stems
    ▶prostrate and leafless or with one bract; MT, WY, UT————**Pussypaws** p91
    ▶NOT as above; flowers
      ▶tiny; dangling red-winged fruits obvious ————**Alpine Sorrel** p87
      ▶with yellow or red eye and shaped like this ————**Primrose Family** p93
      ▶with four petals; fruit usually developing
       on stem below flowers————————————**Mustard Family** p48
      ▶with six petals and sticky glandular stem————**Sticky Tofieldia** p81
      ▶in tight spike with stamens protruding; leaves
       ▶in tightly matted rosettes————————————**Rockmat** p102
       ▶with long petioles, loosely matted————————**Alumroot** p114
      ▶NOT as above————————————————**Saxifrage Family** p111
▶**Some leaves compound or very deeply lobed;** leaflets
  ▶in multiples of three, AND
    ▶shaped like this ————————————**Sibbaldia** p106
    ▶shaped like this ————————**Alpine Meadowrue** p99
  ▶NOT multiples of three, AND are
    ▶finely divided————————————————**Parsley Family** p18
    ▶coarsely and irregularly lobed————————**Valerian Family** p127

►**Stamens of individual flower too many to readily count, collectively easy to see;** petals number

    ►four (rarely six); sepals two or three, fall early————**Poppy Family** p84

    ►five or more; sepals

        ►appear united at base and may appear to be ten due to five bracts alternating with the sepals————**Rose Family** p102
        ►separate at base (sepals may be petal-like)————**Buttercup Family** p95

►**Stamens of individual flower few (ten or less) OR hard to see;** petals number

    ►four————————————————next page
    ►five————————————————page 12

    ►six; sepals

        ►number two (easy to see)————————**Purslane Family** p91

        ►appear absent————————————**Lily Family** p79

    ►seven or eight————————————**Pygmy Bitterroot** p92

    ►ten————————————————**Starwort** p59

►**Leaves opposite (at least lower leaves) OR whorled;** flowers

   ►greenish white and look like this ———————**Monument Plant** p73

   ►pink or white, blue or purple———————**Evening Primrose Family** p82

   ►yellow———————**Weakstem Stonecrop** p62

►**Leaves alternate or entirely basal;** stamens

   ►four———————**Pussypaws** p91

   ►six———————**Mustard Family** p48

   ►eight———————**Evening Primrose Family** p82

   ►ten———————**Stonecrop Family** p62

►**Sepals two (easily seen)**————————————————**Purslane Family** p91

►**Sepals OR sepal lobes ≥ five OR
not easily seen;** stem leaves
 ►alternate OR leaves entirely basal ————————————next page

 ►opposite OR whorled; flowers
  ►dull purple or dull blue————————————————**Star Gentian** p73

  ►white————————————————————————**Pink Family** p57

  ►yellow————————————————**Weakstem Stonecrop** p62

  ►pink; sepals
   ►separate; flowers per stem
    ►one————————————————**Purple Saxifrage** p111
    ►many in head-like raceme————————**Stonecrop Family** p62

   ►united————————————————————**Pink Family** p57

▶**Leaves simple (may be toothed or lobed); stem**
  ▶leafy (at least one leaf on stem); flowers
    ▶sky blue————————————————————————**Blue Flax** p82
    ▶dull blue OR dull purple, star-shaped——————————**Star Gentian** p73
    ▶yellow, white, greenish, pink, crimson OR bright
      red-purple; petals with
      ▶pointed tips, yellow, pink OR crimson; five separate
        pistils; leaves fleshy—————————————**Stonecrop Family** p62
      ▶rounded or blunt tips, yellow, white, greenish OR
        red-purple; ovary topped by two horns 🌷———**Saxifrage Family** p111
  ▶leafless; flowers
    ▶with only two sepals (easily seen)————————**Purslane Family** p91
    ▶pointed like a dart or rocket ⟡————————————**Shooting Star** p94
    ▶NOT as above————————————————————**Saxifrage Family** p111
▶**Leaves compound; leaflets**

  ▶three and shaped like this 🦋————————————————**Sibbaldia** p106

  ▶numerous and appear whorled————————————————**Gordon's Ivesia** p108

  ▶shaped like this 🍁; bulblets replace some flowers————**Woodland Star** p113

14 Key to Plants with Large, Regular Flowers and United Petals

Petals obviously united with a distinct tube topped by petal lobes.
Count lobes to determine number of petals, but don't count sepals.

►**Stem leaves alternate OR leaves entirely basal** next page

►**Stem leaves opposite (at least lower ones), AND**
  ►compound or deeply lobed —————————————— **Valerian Family** p127
  ►NOT as above; flowers

  ►urn-shaped or bowl-shape ———————————— **Heath Family** p63

  ►phlox type with lobes opened flat,
   perpendicular to narrow tube ————————————— **Phlox** p85

  ►small, white, numerous, with 3 stamens ————————— **Valerian Family** p127

  ►NOT as above ——————————————————————— **Gentian Family** p73

►**Stem leaves densely covering stem AND**
  needle- or scale-like; flowers
  ►urn- (see above) or bell-shaped ———————————— **Heath Family** p63
  ►NOT as above ——————————————————————— **Phlox** p85

► **Stem leaves absent**; petals

   ► four————————————————————————**Lapland Gentian** p74

   ► five————————————————————————**Primrose Family** p93

► **Stem leaves present, AND**

   ► some are compound OR very deeply
   lobed and appear compound; plant

      ► with stamens much longer than petals; flowers pale
      lavender to purple; inflorescence
      OR its branches may be curled—————————**Waterleaf Family** p78

      ► NOT as above; flowers

         ► greenish yellow————————————————**Gordon's Ivesia** p108

         ► white, blue or purple—————————————**Phlox Family** p85

   ► simple (may be lobed but not so deeply as
   to be confused with a compound leaf); flowers

     ► urn-shaped like this ————————————————**Heath Family** p63

     ► NOT urn-shaped—————————————————next page

►**Flowers blue to purple, bell-like
with pointed lobes, ovary inferior**——————————**Bellflower Family** p56

►**Flowers NOT as above (OR if blue then with
rounded lobes), ovary superior; flowers**
  ►with an eye (opening at top of tube ringed by bumps
  of somewhat different color) OR bell-shaped like this

  AND usually blue; ovary or fruit four-lobed——————**Borage Family** p46

  ►without distinct eye AND with petals white, pink or
  shades of blue; ovary not lobed; leaf

  ►spoon- or fan-shaped——————————————**Alpine Collomia** p85

  ►NOT as above; stamens
    ►obviously protrude from corolla tube;
    inflorescence or its branches
    curled in bud like a scorpion's tail————**Waterleaf Family** p78

    ►hidden or only slightly protruding; inflorescence
    congested or nodding but NOT curled———————**Phlox Family** p85

►**Leaves simple, entire or toothed;** flower

  ►resembles garden violet 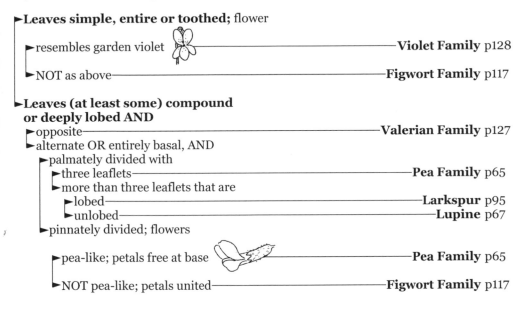 ————————————————**Violet Family** p128

  ►NOT as above————————————————————————**Figwort Family** p117

►**Leaves (at least some) compound
or deeply lobed AND**

  ►opposite————————————————————————————**Valerian Family** p127

  ►alternate OR entirely basal, AND

    ►palmately divided with

      ►three leaflets————————————————————————**Pea Family** p65

      ►more than three leaflets that are

        ►lobed————————————————————————**Larkspur** p95

        ►unlobed——————————————————————**Lupine** p67

    ►pinnately divided; flowers

      ►pea-like; petals free at base ——————————**Pea Family** p65

      ►NOT pea-like; petals united————————————————**Figwort Family** p117

> **PARSLEY or CARROT FAMILY**
> (*Apiaceae* or *Umbelliferae*) Herbs with tiny
> flowers in umbels. Flower parts in fives,
> petals separate, ovary inferior. Leaves
> usually compound.

Parsley Family members are numerous and
difficult to identify. A few common and/or
distinctive species are included here.

►Leaves simple
  American Thoroughwort
  Bupleurum americanum
  (*B. triradiatum*)

►Leaves compound; flowers
  ► yellow, next page

  ► NOT yellow, page 20

yellow-brown-purple

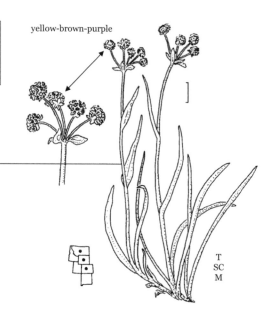

T
SC
M

►Plant showy, usually > 10cm
(4in) tall; anise or celery odor
when crushed
  Rocky Mountain Parsley
  Cymopterus longilobus
  (*C. hendersonii*)

all yellow

►Plant tiny, usually < 10cm (4in) tall
  Alpine Parsley
  Oreoxis alpina
  (bracts entire; fruits minutely hairy;
  widespread but not on Pike's Peak, CO)

  Baker's Alpine Parsley, *O. bakeri*, toothed
  bracts often purplish, swCO, NM, UT;
  Dwarf Alpine Parsley, *O. humilis*, entire
  greenish bracts, fruits not hairy, Pike's
  Peak, CO; **Yellow Mountain Parsley**,
  Cymopterus lemmonii, (*Pseudocymopterus
  montanus*), stem leaves usually present,
  sometimes taller than 10cm, CO, NM,
  WY, UT; other species hard to separate.

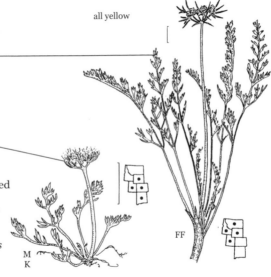

M
K

FF

►Plant low, under 15cm (6in) tall,
mat- or clump-forming; leaf lobes
tiny, less than 2mm wide
  Fernleaf Spring Parsley——————————————
  Cymopterus bipinnatus
  (leaves gray, tightly bunched;
  leaves all basal)

  Cusick's Lomatium, *Lomatium cusickii*,
  leaves green, stem leaves usually present,
  ID, MT; **Long-stem Parsley,** *Cymopterus*
  longipes, leaves gray, loosely bunched,
  ID, UT, WY.

►Plant usually much taller,
few-stemmed with obvious stem
leaves; leaf lobes > 5mm wide, next page

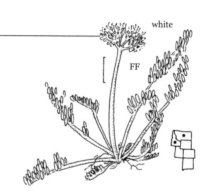

white

FF

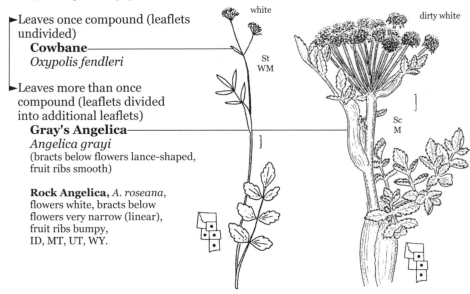

►Leaves once compound (leaflets undivided)
Cowbane
Oxypolis fendleri

white

St
WM

dirty white

►Leaves more than once compound (leaflets divided into additional leaflets)
Gray's Angelica
Angelica grayi
(bracts below flowers lance-shaped, fruit ribs smooth)

Sc
M

Rock Angelica, *A. roseana*,
flowers white, bracts below
flowers very narrow (linear),
fruit ribs bumpy,
ID, MT, UT, WY.

SUNFLOWER or ASTER FAMILY
(*Asteraceae* or *Compositae*) Large family with small flowers tightly grouped into heads subtended by bracts. Flowers of two types, ray and disk. Sepals modified into bristles or scales called pappus.

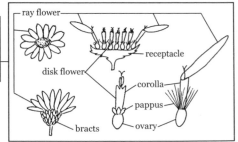

- Heads with BOTH ray and disk flowers (daisy or sunflower-like); rays
  - yellow or orange, page 30
  - NOT yellow or orange, page 40
- Heads with disk flowers ONLY (button, thistle, tassel or furry pussytoe-like), page 25
- Heads with ray flowers ONLY (dandelion-like); flowers
  - yellow, next page
  - orange

Burnt-orange Dandelion

Agoseris aurantiaca
(outer bracts mostly green and < 3mm)
A. aurantiaca var. *purpurea*
(outer bracts purple-blotched, > 3mm wide near middle)

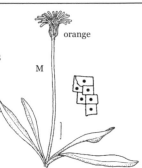

▶Bracts with black hairs
   Alpine Hawkweed
   Hieracium gracile
   (*Chlorocrepis tristis* ssp. *gracile*)

▶Bracts NOT as above; plant with
  ▶ several heads
    Dwarf Hawksbeard
    Crepis nana (*Askellia*)
  ▶ one head; bracts
    ▶ in two rows, outer shorter
     than inner, fruit
     knobby at apex, next page

    ▶ graded in length or almost equal
     from outer to inner, fruit smooth
     False Dandelion
     Agoseris glauca

    Woolly-headed Dandelion, *A. glauca* var.
dasycephala, large head and woolly bracts,
same range as *A. glauca*.

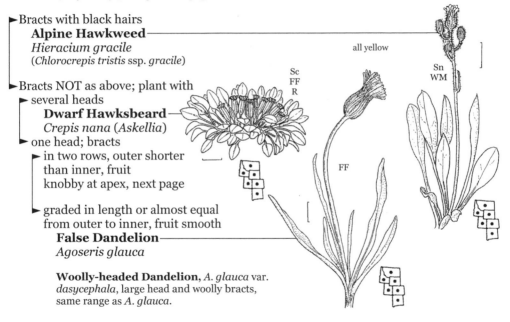

all yellow

Sc
FF
R

Sn
WM

FF

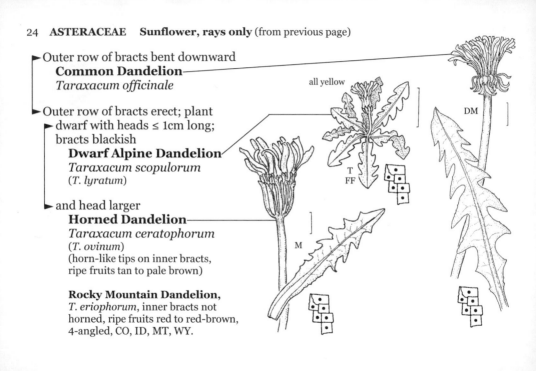

▶ Outer row of bracts bent downward
Common Dandelion
Taraxacum officinale

all yellow

DM

▶ Outer row of bracts erect; plant
▶ dwarf with heads ≤ 1cm long;
bracts blackish
Dwarf Alpine Dandelion
Taraxacum scopulorum
(*T. lyratum*)

T
FF

▶ and head larger
Horned Dandelion
Taraxacum ceratophorum
(*T. ovinum*)
(horn-like tips on inner bracts,
ripe fruits tan to pale brown)

M

Rocky Mountain Dandelion,
T. eriophorum, inner bracts not
horned, ripe fruits red to red-brown,
4-angled, CO, ID, MT, WY.

►Plant NOT spiny, next page

►Plant spiny; flower heads

   ► congested, top heavy
    and nodding
     Alpine Thistle
     Cirsium scopulorum
     (flowers yellow in sCO)

   ► in tight terminal clusters,
   not or only slightly nodding
    Tweedy's Thistle
    Cirsium eatonii
    (*C. tweedyi*)

    Colorado Thistle, *C. scariosum,*
    (*C. coloradense, C. tioganum* var.
    coloradense),whitish, sometimes
    stemless, in damp meadows,
    CO, NM, WY.

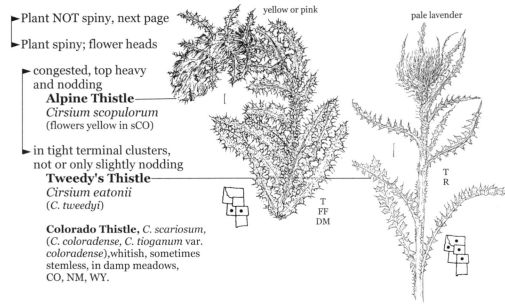

yellow or pink

pale lavender

T
FF
DM

T
R

pale yellow

▶Leaves NOT divided, page 28

▶Leaves (at least some) divided; heads

▶ one to sometimes four per stem, next page

▶ usually more than four per stem
   Rocky Mountain Sage —————
   Artemisia scopulorum
   (bract edges brown, receptacle hairy,
   flower lobes hairy)

   Boreal Sage, *A. campestris* ssp. *borealis*
   (*A. campestris* var. *purshii, Oligosporus*
   groenlandicus), heads small, receptacle not
   hairy, stems reddish, bract edges light colored,
   CO, ID, MT, WY;
   Michaux's Sage, *A. michauxiana*, leaves green
   with very strong odor, CO, ID, MT, UT, WY;
   Arctic Sage, *A. norvegica* var. *saxicola* (*A. arctica*),
   heads large, receptacle not hairy, flowers hairy
   externally, bract edges dark, CO, ID, MT, WY.

DM

►Flowers white to pink
   Alpine Dusty Maiden
   Chaenactis alpina

white to pink

T
R
FF
Sc

►Flowers yellow
   Gold Buttons
   Erigeron compositus
   var. *discoideus*
   (rayless form)

yellow

R
FF
DM

Few-headed Sage, *Artemisia pattersonii*, bract edges dark brown, leaves divided only once, smell like sage, heads 1 - 4, flower lobes not hairy, CO, NM, WY.

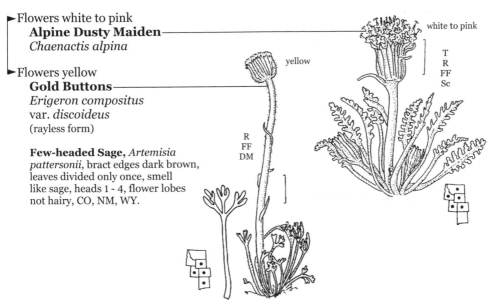

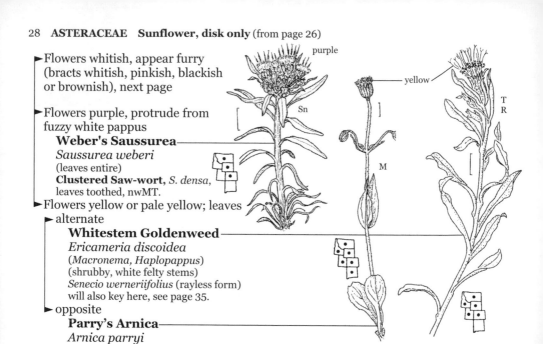

►Flowers whitish, appear furry (bracts whitish, pinkish, blackish or brownish), next page

►Flowers purple, protrude from fuzzy white pappus
  Weber's Saussurea
  Saussurea weberi
  (leaves entire)
  Clustered Saw-wort, *S. densa*, leaves toothed, nwMT.

►Flowers yellow or pale yellow; leaves
  ►alternate
    Whitestem Goldenweed
    Ericameria discoidea
    (*Macronema, Haplopappus*)
    (shrubby, white felty stems)
    Senecio werneriifolius (rayless form) will also key here, see page 35.
  ►opposite
    Parry's Arnica
    Arnica parryi

purple

yellow

Sn

M

T
R

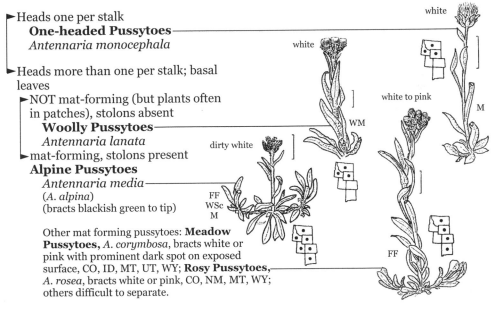

►Heads one per stalk
　One-headed Pussytoes
　　Antennaria monocephala

white

white

►Heads more than one per stalk; basal
leaves
　►NOT mat-forming (but plants often
　in patches), stolons absent
　　Woolly Pussytoes
　　　Antennaria lanata

white to pink

M

WM

dirty white

　►mat-forming, stolons present
　　Alpine Pussytoes
　　　Antennaria media
　　　(*A. alpina*)
　　　(bracts blackish green to tip)

FF
WSc
M

Other mat forming pussytoes: **Meadow
Pussytoes,** *A. corymbosa*, bracts white or
pink with prominent dark spot on exposed
surface, CO, ID, MT, UT, WY; **Rosy Pussytoes,**
A. rosea, bracts white or pink, CO, NM, MT, WY;
others difficult to separate.

FF

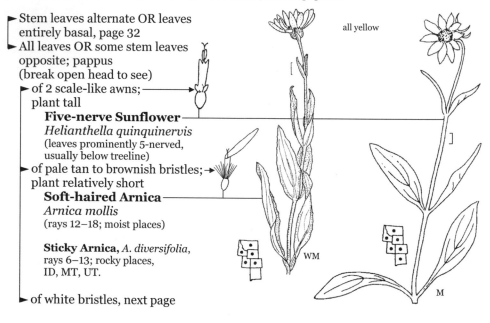

▶ Stem leaves alternate OR leaves
  entirely basal, page 32
▶ All leaves OR some stem leaves
  opposite; pappus
  (break open head to see)
  ▶ of 2 scale-like awns;
    plant tall
    Five-nerve Sunflower
    Helianthella quinquinervis
    (leaves prominently 5-nerved,
    usually below treeline)
  ▶ of pale tan to brownish bristles;
    plant relatively short
    Soft-haired Arnica
    Arnica mollis
    (rays 12–18; moist places)

    Sticky Arnica, *A. diversifolia,*
    rays 6–13; rocky places,
    ID, MT, UT.

▶ of white bristles, next page

all yellow

WM

M

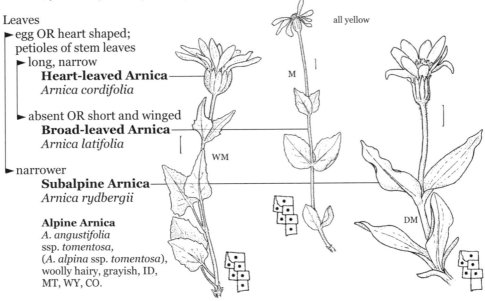

Leaves
► egg OR heart shaped;
petioles of stem leaves
    ► long, narrow
       Heart-leaved Arnica
       Arnica cordifolia

    ► absent OR short and winged
       Broad-leaved Arnica
       Arnica latifolia

► narrower
       Subalpine Arnica
       Arnica rydbergii

Alpine Arnica
A. angustifolia
ssp. *tomentosa*,
(*A. alpina* ssp. *tomentosa*),
woolly hairy, grayish, ID,
MT, WY, CO.

all yellow

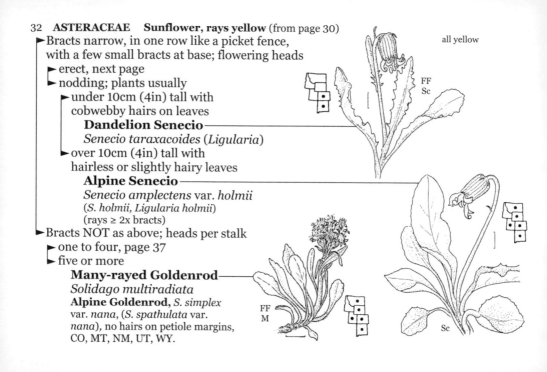

▶ Bracts narrow, in one row like a picket fence,
with a few small bracts at base; flowering heads
   ▶ erect, next page
   ▶ nodding; plants usually
      ▶ under 10cm (4in) tall with
      cobwebby hairs on leaves
        Dandelion Senecio——
        Senecio taraxacoides (*Ligularia*)
      ▶ over 10cm (4in) tall with
      hairless or slightly hairy leaves
        Alpine Senecio——
        Senecio amplectens var. *holmii*
        (*S. holmii, Ligularia holmii*)
        (rays ≥ 2x bracts)
▶ Bracts NOT as above; heads per stalk
   ▶ one to four, page 37
   ▶ five or more
      Many-rayed Goldenrod——
      Solidago multiradiata
      Alpine Goldenrod, *S. simplex*
      var. *nana*, (*S. spathulata* var.
      nana), no hairs on petiole margins,
      CO, MT, NM, UT, WY.

all yellow

FF
Sc

FF
M

Sc

▶ Leaf blade green or purple,
hairless or sparsely hairy, next page

▶ Leaf blade gray-hairy; stems
  ▶ tall with large
    lance-shaped leaves
      Black-Tipped Senecio
      Senecio atratus

  ▶ short, < 30cm (12in) tall;
    stem leaves
    ▶ bract-like; rays yellow
      Woolly Senecio
      Packera cana
      (*Senecio canus, S. harbourii*)
      (plant somewhat hairy)
    ▶ large; rays orange
      Twice-hairy Senecio
      Senecio fuscatus
      (*S. lindstroemii*)
      (plant densely hairy)

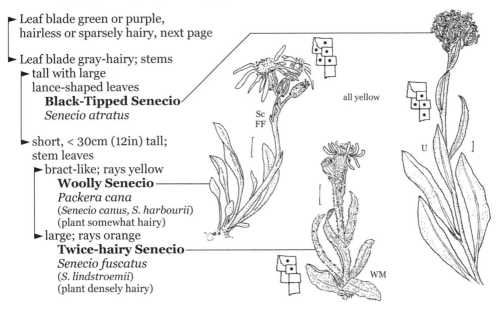

Sc FF

all yellow

U]

WM

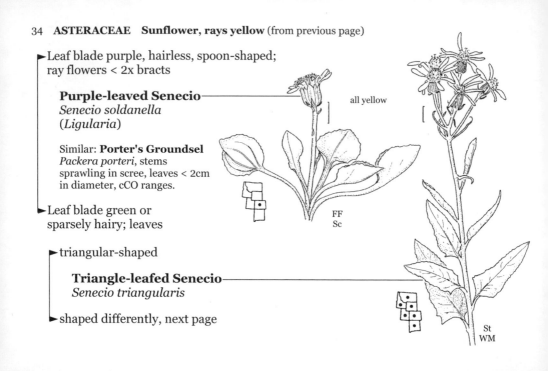

►Leaf blade purple, hairless, spoon-shaped;
ray flowers < 2x bracts

Purple-leaved Senecio
Senecio soldanella
(*Ligularia*)

Similar: **Porter's Groundsel**
Packera porteri, stems
sprawling in scree, leaves < 2cm
in diameter, cCO ranges.

all yellow

►Leaf blade green or
sparsely hairy; leaves

►triangular-shaped

Triangle-leafed Senecio
Senecio triangularis

►shaped differently, next page

FF
Sc

St
WM

► Stem leaves prominent AND basal
leaves small or withered, next page
► Stem leaves present, clasping stem
AND basal leaves well developed, tufted

Saffron Senecio
Packera crocatus (*Senecio*)
(flowers usually orange, middle stem
leaves < basal leaves, not lobed at base)

Similar: **Two-leafed Senecio,**
P. dimorphophyllus, flowers usually yellow,
middle stem leaves > basal leaves and
with lobed base, dry meadows,
slopes and rock crevices, all states.

► Stem leaves absent OR reduced to bracts

Rocky Senecio
Packera werneriifolia (*Senecio*)
(loose mats on scree and cliffs, flowers yellow)
Similar: **Rocky Mt. Butterweed,**
P. streptanthifolia , flowers yellow,
wet meadows, all states;
Dwarf Arctic Ragweed, *P. cymbalaria*,
(*Senecio residifolius*), disk flowers orange, fellfields, MT.

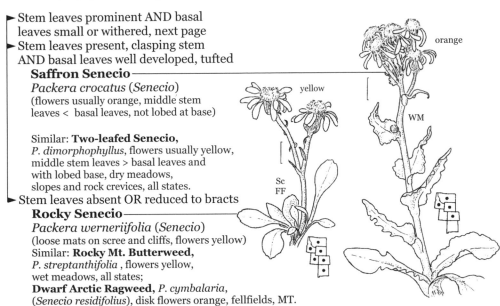

►Leaves sharply toothed, hairless
Dwarf Mountain-butterweed
Senecio fremontii var. *blitoides*

Similar: *S. fremontii* var. *fremontii*,
neUT, cWY.

►Leaves slightly toothed OR entire
Mountain Meadow Groundsel
Butterweed
Senecio crassulus
(hairless)

Lambstongue Senecio,
S. integerrimus var. *exaltatus,*
leaves entire, plant hairy,
ID, NM, UT, WY.

all yellow

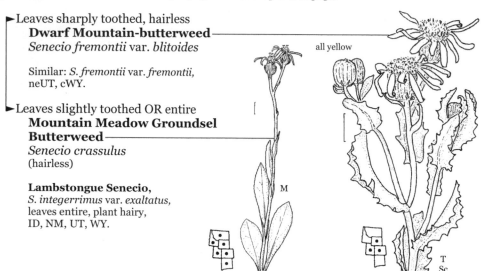

▶Petals ALL obviously three-toothed like this;
stems
  ▶leafless
    Goldflower
    Tetraneuris acaulis var. *caespitosa*
    (*Tetraneuris brevifolia, Hymenoyxs*)

  ▶leafy
    Old-Man-of-the-Mountain
    Tetraneuris grandiflora
    (*Rydbergia, Hymenoyxs*)
    (all basal leaves 3 - 5 lobed)

    Rydberg's Daisy, *T. brandegei*, some
    basal leaves entire, replaces *T. grandiflora*
    in sCO & nNM.

▶Petal teeth tiny or absent; stem leaves
  ▶well developed, next page
  ▶bract-like, sparse
    Stemless Goldenweed
    Stenotus acaulis (*Haplopappus*)

all yellow

►Leaves toothed
Alpine Hulsea————————————————————————————
Hulsea algida   all yellow

Hoary Balsamroot,
Balsamorhiza incana, leaves
deeply lobed, ID, seMT to wcWY.

►Leaves entire, sometimes
wavy edged; plant
  ►an obvious shrub with woody,
  white stems
    Shrubby Goldenweed——
    Ericameria suffruticosa
    (*Haplopappus*)

  ►an herb with many stems forming
  neat roundish mounds
    Golden Aster————
    Heterotheca pumila (*Chrysopsis*)

►NOT as above, next page

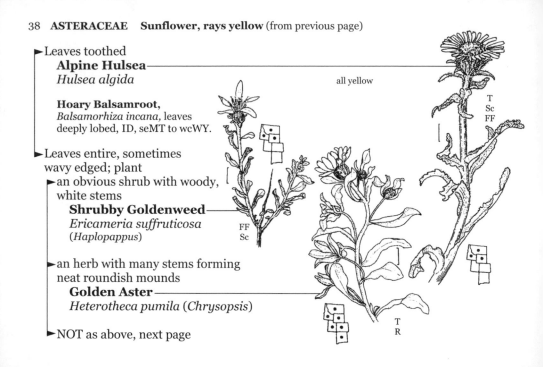

► Leaves covered with matted,
   woolly hairs
      Woolly Goldenweed
      Stenotus lanuginosa
      (*Haplopappus*)
► Leaves NOT woolly or glandular
      Dwarf Goldenweed
      Tonestus pygmaeus
      (*Haplopappus*)
      (small cushion, common on
      gravelly or rocky tundra)
      Plantain Goldenweed, *Pyrrocoma
      uniflora* (*Haplopappus*), plant stems
      few, sprawling, flowers showy, rare in
      gravelly meadows, all states but NM.
► Leaves covered with gland tipped,

   pinhead hairs
      Lyall's Goldenweed
      Tonestus lyallii
      (*Haplopappus*)
      (loose mat, uncommon on
      unstable slopes or steep tundra)

all yellow

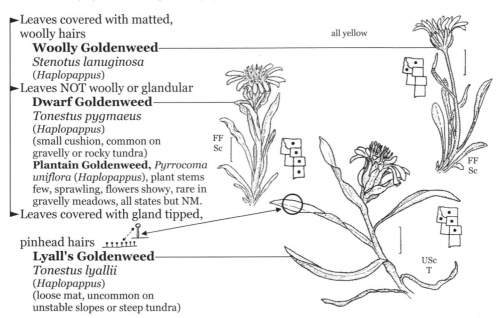

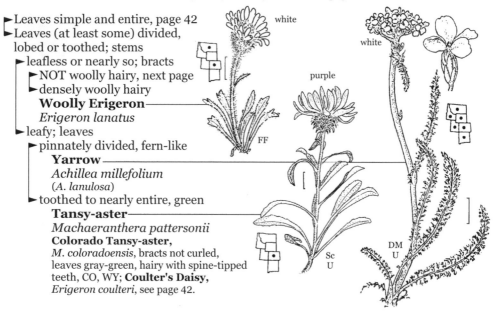

►Leaves simple and entire, page 42
►Leaves (at least some) divided,
lobed or toothed; stems
  ►leafless or nearly so; bracts
    ►NOT woolly hairy, next page
    ►densely woolly hairy
    Woolly Erigeron———
    Erigeron lanatus
  ►leafy; leaves
    ►pinnately divided, fern-like
    Yarrow———
    Achillea millefolium
    (*A. lanulosa*)
    ►toothed to nearly entire, green
    Tansy-aster———
    Machaeranthera pattersonii
    Colorado Tansy-aster,
    M. coloradoensis, bracts not curled,
    leaves gray-green, hairy with spine-tipped
    teeth, CO, WY; **Coulter's Daisy,**
    Erigeron coulteri, see page 42.

white

white

purple

FF

Sc
U

DM
U

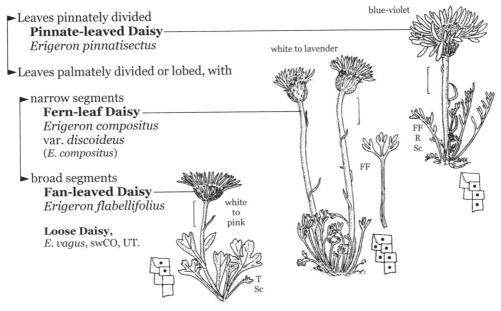

►Leaves pinnately divided
   Pinnate-leaved Daisy
   Erigeron pinnatisectus

blue-violet

white to lavender

►Leaves palmately divided or lobed, with

►narrow segments
   Fern-leaf Daisy
   Erigeron compositus
   var. *discoideus*
   (*E. compositus*)

►broad segments
   Fan-leaved Daisy
   Erigeron flabellifolius

   Loose Daisy,
   E. vagus, swCO, UT.

white
to
pink

FF
R
Sc

FF

T
Sc

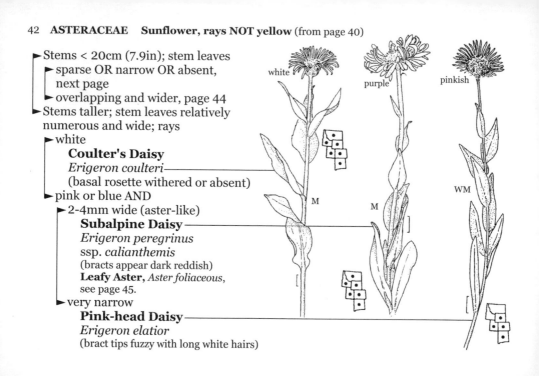

►Stems < 20cm (7.9in); stem leaves
   ► sparse OR narrow OR absent,
   next page
   ► overlapping and wider, page 44
►Stems taller; stem leaves relatively
numerous and wide; rays
  ► white
     Coulter's Daisy
     Erigeron coulteri——
     (basal rosette withered or absent)
  ► pink or blue AND
    ► 2-4mm wide (aster-like)
      Subalpine Daisy——
      Erigeron peregrinus
      ssp. *calianthemis*
      (bracts appear dark reddish)
      Leafy Aster, *Aster foliaceous,*
      see page 45.
  ► very narrow
     Pink-head Daisy——
     Erigeron elatior
     (bract tips fuzzy with long white hairs)

white

purple

pinkish

M

M

WM

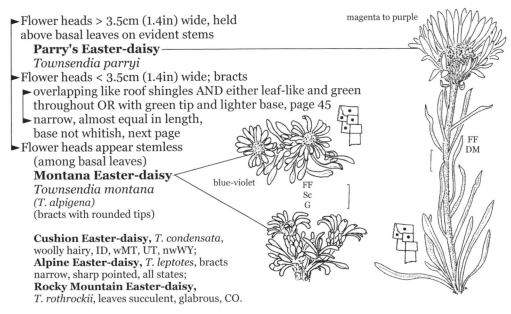

magenta to purple

►Flower heads > 3.5cm (1.4in) wide, held above basal leaves on evident stems
   Parry's Easter-daisy —————
   Townsendia parryi
►Flower heads < 3.5cm (1.4in) wide; bracts
   ►overlapping like roof shingles AND either leaf-like and green throughout OR with green tip and lighter base, page 45
   ►narrow, almost equal in length, base not whitish, next page
►Flower heads appear stemless (among basal leaves)
   Montana Easter-daisy
   Townsendia montana
   (T. alpigena)
   (bracts with rounded tips)

blue-violet

FF
Sc
G

FF
DM

Cushion Easter-daisy, *T. condensata*, woolly hairy, ID, wMT, UT, nwWY;
Alpine Easter-daisy, *T. leptotes*, bracts narrow, sharp pointed, all states;
Rocky Mountain Easter-daisy, *T. rothrockii*, leaves succulent, glabrous, CO.

▶Rays violet, blue, or purple
One-headed Daisy————————
Erigeron simplex
(bracts white-woolly, basal rosette present)

blue (white)

Many other species difficult to separate:
Rockslide Daisy, *E. leiomerus,* rock crevices and
ledges, bracts reddish glandular, all states; **Bear Daisy,**
E. ursinus, meadows, patch-forming, bracts with
reddish tips and some white hairs, base of stem
purple and strongly curved, all but NM; **Rough Daisy,**
E. asperuginus, ridges, cID, wMT; **Rydberg's Daisy,**
E. rydbergii, leaves < 3mm wide, cID, swMT, nwWY;
Leafy Aster, *Aster foliaceous*, bracts leaf-like with
enlarged green tips and ciliate margins, see page 45.

white

M

▶Rays white
Black-headed Daisy————————
Erigeron melanocephalus
(basal rosette of spoon-shaped leaves, bracts dark-hairy)

Sn
WSc

Arctic-Alpine Daisy, *E. humilis,* tiny, rays short, hardly spreading,
rare in mossy tundra, CO, cID, nwMT, UT, nWY; **Evermann's Daisy,**
E. evermannii, stem leafless, very unstable talus, cID, wMT.

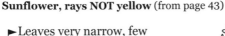

► Leaves very narrow, few
　　Alpine Aster
　　Aster alpigenus
　　(*Oreostemma*)

　　Rocky Mountain Aster,
　　A. stenomeres (*Ionactis*),
　　stems leafy, ID, MT.
► Leaves wider AND
　► hairless or nearly so
　　　Leafy Aster
　　　Aster foliaceous var. *apricus*
　　　(*Symphytotrichum*)
　　　(bracts leaflike with enlarged green
　　　tips and ciliate margins)
　► short hairy
　　　Arctic Aster
　　　Aster sibiricus var. *meritus*
　　　(rays purple, stems leafy)

　　Alp Aster, *A. alpinus* var. *vierhapperi,*
　　(*Ionactis*) rays white to pale lavender,
　　stem leaves reduced, rare, CO.

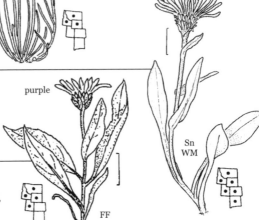

purple

pink to purple

WSc
M

purple

Sn
WM

FF

BORAGE FAMILY (*Boraginaceae*) Flowers regular
with five partially united petals, which form a tube.
Ovary superior, four-lobed. Leaves simple, usually alternate.

► Flowers white; plant stiff hairy
  Alpine Cryptantha———————————————
  Cryptantha sobolifera
  (*C. nubigena, C. hypsophila*)
► Flowers blue (rarely white); corolla lobes
  ► NOT perpendicular to tube, next page

  ► perpendicular to tube; plant
    ► mat forming
      Alpine Forget-me-not———
      Eritrichum nanum
      var. *elongatum*
      (*E. aretioides*)
      (occasionally white flowered)

    ► NOT mat forming
      Woods Forget-me-not————————————————
      Myosotis alpestris (*M. asiatica*)

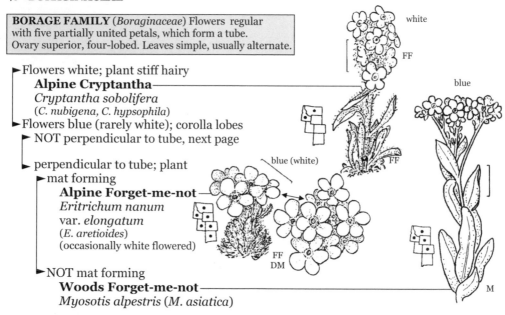

white

FF

blue

FF

blue (white)

FF
DM

M

►Leaves with several lateral
veins, wet or moist areas
  Tall Chiming Bells
  Mertensia ciliata

►Leaves with few or no
lateral veins, drier
areas; anthers

  ►hidden in tube
    Alpine Chiming Bells
    Mertensia alpina

  ►NOT hidden in tube
    Green-leaf Chiming Bells
    Mertensia viridis
    (*M. lanceolata*)

all blue

T
Sn
M

St

FF
DM

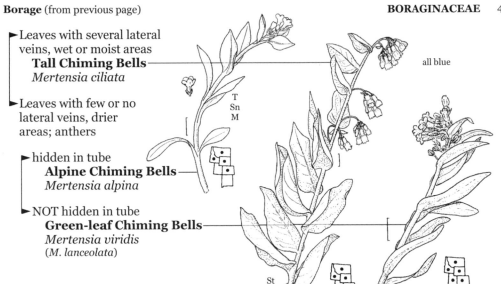

MUSTARD FAMILY (*Brassicaceae* or *Cruciferae*)
Flowers regular with four sepals, four
petals, six stamens, superior ovary. Diverse
leaf hairs useful for species identification.

►Flowers yellow, page 52

►Flowers white, pink or purple; leaves

  ► simple, next page

  ► compound; plant

    ►gray hairy
      Alpine Smelowskia
      Smelowskia calycina
      var. *americana*

    ►NOT gray hairy
      Small Brookcress
      Cardamine pennsylvanica
      (infrequent)

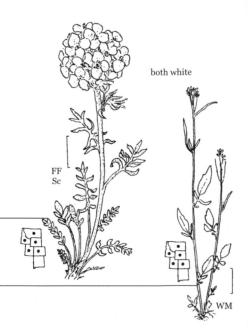

both white

FF
Sc

WM

►Flowers usually white, next page
►Flowers maroon, burnt orange
 or purple, large
    Wallflower
    Erysimum capitatum
    (stem leaves more than one)

    Parrya, *Parrya nudicaulis,* flowers
    few in head, usually purple, stem
    leaves none or one, WY, ID;
    Uinta Parrya, *P. rydbergii,* lavender
    flowers, toothed leaves, Uinta Mts, UT.

►Flowers pink, small
    Lyall's Rockcress
    Boechera lyallii (*Arabis*)
    [Plant < 15cm (6in) tall, basal
    leaves hairless or nearly so.]
    Lemmon's Rockcress, *B. lemmonii,*
    plant < 15cm tall; basal leaves
    grayish-hairy, late snowmelt areas;
    Drummond's Rockcress, *B. drummondii,*
    plant > 15cm tall, leaves sparsely hairy
    with pick-shaped hairs, usually below treeline.

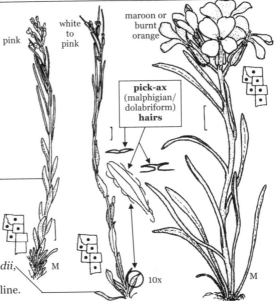

pink

white
to
pink

maroon or
burnt
orange

pick-ax
(malphigian/
dolabriform)
hairs

M

10x

M

►Plant of wet areas
    Brookcress————————————————
    Cardamine cordifolia

►Plant of drier areas; leaves
    ►clasping stem
        Mountain Candytuff————
        Noccea montana
        (*T. alpestre, T. montanum*)

    ►NOT clasping stem or absent;
    seed pod
        ►at least ten times longer
        than wide
            Rockcress————————
            Boechera nuttallii
            (*Arabis*)

    ►shorter, next page

all white

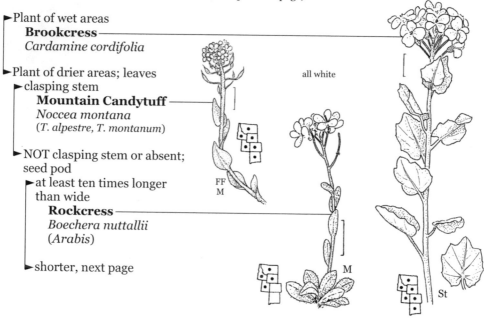

FF
M

M

St

► Stem leaves two or more; stellate to dendritic hairs
  White Draba
  Draba breweri var. *cana*
  (*D. cana*, *D. lanceolata*)
  (style 0.25-0.4mm, leaf-like bract
  below some flowers, fruit erect)
  Northern Rockcress, *D. borealis*,
  style 0.5-1mm, flowers not bracted,
  uncommon, CO, WY; **Smith
  Whitlow-grass,** *D. smithii*, style
  1.5-2mm, rare, sCO.
► Stem leaves absent OR one;
  basal leaves
  ► NOT hairy; leaf margins ciliate
  with simple stiff hairs
    Arctic Draba
    Draba fladnizensis
  ► hairy with forked hairs
    Longfruit Draba
    Draba lonchocarpa (*D. nivalis*)
    (hairs dense, many stellate with 8 rays)
    D. porsildii, hairs loose with 3-5 rays,
    mostly cruciform; uncommon, CO, WY.

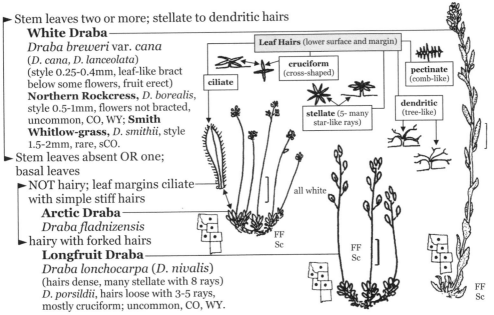

Leaf Hairs (lower surface and margin)

ciliate

cruciform
(cross-shaped)

pectinate
(comb-like)

stellate (5- many
star-like rays)

dendritic
(tree-like)

all white

FF
Sc

FF
Sc

FF
Sc

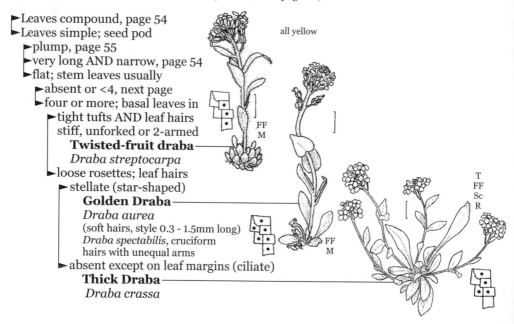

►Leaves compound, page 54
►Leaves simple; seed pod
  ►plump, page 55
  ►very long AND narrow, page 54
  ►flat; stem leaves usually
    ►absent or <4, next page
    ►four or more; basal leaves in
      ►tight tufts AND leaf hairs
       stiff, unforked or 2-armed
      Twisted-fruit draba
      Draba streptocarpa
    ►loose rosettes; leaf hairs
      ►stellate (star-shaped)
      Golden Draba
      Draba aurea
      (soft hairs, style 0.3 - 1.5mm long)
      Draba spectabilis, cruciform
      hairs with unequal arms
      ►absent except on leaf margins (ciliate)
      Thick Draba
      Draba crassa

all yellow

FF
M

FF
M

T
FF
Sc
R

►Hairs four to many-forked or -rayed (look at lower leaf surface); plant mat forming

Mat Draba

Draba oligosperma
(likes limestone, hairs sessile, mostly <u>pectinate</u>)

all yellow

D. incerta, hairs stalked, mostly dendritic, all states
but NM); *D. ventosa*, (hairs dense, dendritic,
long-stalked, style 1-1.5mm, all but NM)

►Hairs unbranched or few-forked; style

►obscure, < 0.15mm

Thick-leaved or Snowbed Draba

Draba crassifolia
(tiny, basal leaves ciliate or not hairy)
D. albertina, some branched hairs , all states

►evident, > 0.2mm; basal leaves ciliate

Grays Peak Whitlowgrass

Draba grayana
(stem leaves 1 – 4, dense tangled
unforked and 1–forked hairs on stem)
Other similar species uncommon or local in
distribution: *D. exunguiculata*, sepals clasp fruits, n&cCO;
D. graminea, bracts subtend flowers, CO; *D. globosa*, tiny
incurved basal leaves and no stem leaves, all states but NM.

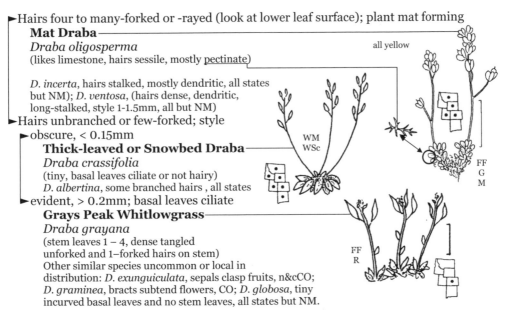

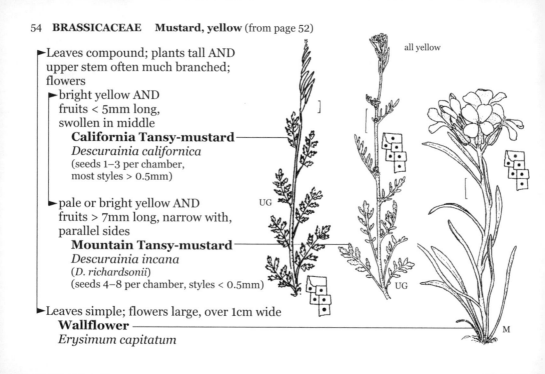

►Leaves compound; plants tall AND
upper stem often much branched;
flowers
  ►bright yellow AND
  fruits < 5mm long,
  swollen in middle
    California Tansy-mustard
    Descurainia californica
    (seeds 1–3 per chamber,
    most styles > 0.5mm)

  ►pale or bright yellow AND
  fruits > 7mm long, narrow with,
  parallel sides
    Mountain Tansy-mustard
    Descurainia incana
    (*D. richardsonii*)
    (seeds 4–8 per chamber, styles < 0.5mm)

►Leaves simple; flowers large, over 1cm wide
  Wallflower
  Erysimum capitatum

all yellow

UG

UG

M

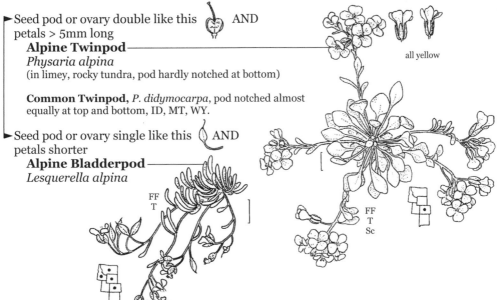

►Seed pod or ovary double like this   AND
petals > 5mm long
    Alpine Twinpod————————————————————
    Physaria alpina
    (in limey, rocky tundra, pod hardly notched at bottom)

    Common Twinpod, *P. didymocarpa,* pod notched almost
    equally at top and bottom, ID, MT, WY.

►Seed pod or ovary single like this   AND
petals shorter
    Alpine Bladderpod————
    Lesquerella alpina

all yellow

FF
T

FF
T
Sc

> **BELLFLOWER FAMILY** (*Campanulaceae*)
> Flowers usually blue or purple and bell-like
> with five united petals and an inferior ovary.
> Leaves alternate, simple.

►Plant less than 5cm (2in) tall; flowers
tiny, narrow; anthers 1.5 - 2.5mm long
  Alpine Harebell
  Campanula uniflora
►Plant more than 5cm (2in) tall; flowers
large; anthers 4 - 6.5mm long; petal lobes
  ►1/3 length of flower; one or more,
  usually nodding, flowers per stem;
  nodding fruit opens by pores at base
    Mountain Harebell
    Campanula rotundifolia
  ►1/2 length of flower; one erect
  flower per stem; erect fruit
  opens by pores at summit
    Parry's Harebell
    Campanula parryi
    Rough Harebell, *C. scabrella*, coarse hairs, fellfields, ID, MT.

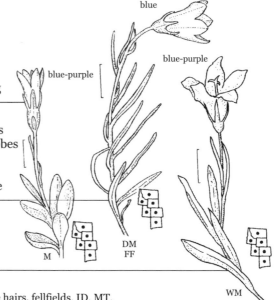

blue

blue-purple

blue-purple

blue-purple

DM
FF

M

WM

PINK FAMILY (*Caryophyllaceae*) Herbs with entire, opposite leaves, stem often with swollen nodes. Flowers regular, petals five, separate, stamens ten, ovary superior.

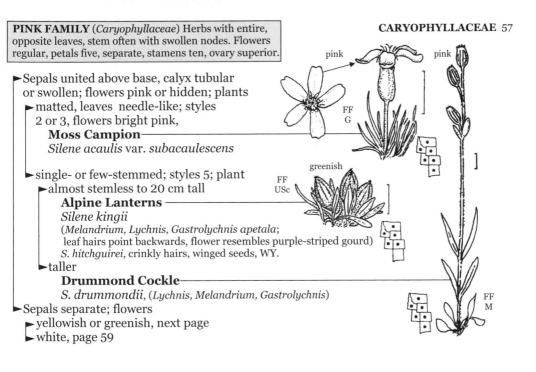

►Sepals united above base, calyx tubular or swollen; flowers pink or hidden; plants
  ►matted, leaves needle-like; styles 2 or 3, flowers bright pink,
    Moss Campion
    Silene acaulis var. *subacaulescens*

  ►single- or few-stemmed; styles 5; plant
    ►almost stemless to 20 cm tall
      Alpine Lanterns
      Silene kingii
      (*Melandrium, Lychnis, Gastrolychnis apetala*;
      leaf hairs point backwards, flower resembles purple-striped gourd)
      S. hitchguirei, crinkly hairs, winged seeds, WY.
    ►taller
      Drummond Cockle
      S. drummondii, (*Lychnis, Melandrium, Gastrolychnis*)

►Sepals separate; flowers
  ►yellowish or greenish, next page
  ►white, page 59

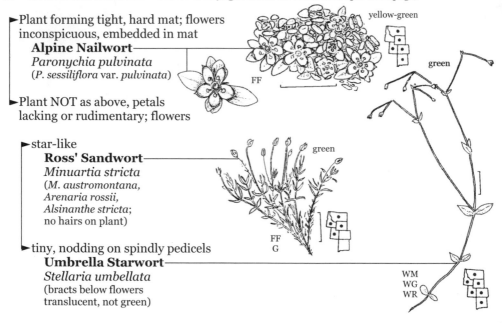

►Plant forming tight, hard mat; flowers
inconspicuous, embedded in mat
  Alpine Nailwort
  Paronychia pulvinata
  (*P. sessiliflora* var. *pulvinata*)

yellow-green

FF

green

►Plant NOT as above, petals
lacking or rudimentary; flowers

  ►star-like
    Ross' Sandwort
    Minuartia stricta
    (*M. austromontana,*
    Arenaria rossii,
    Alsinanthe stricta;
    no hairs on plant)

green

FF
G

  ►tiny, nodding on spindly pedicels
    Umbrella Starwort
    Stellaria umbellata
    (bracts below flowers
    translucent, not green)

WM
WG
WR

►Petals five, entire or not deeply lobed, next page
►Petals five, deeply two lobed OR appear to be ten; plant
  ►with pin-head sticky (glandular) hairs
  (use hand lens to see)

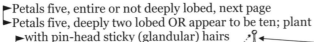

  Alpine Chickweed
  Cerastium beeringianum
  (bracts below inflorescence totally green)
  Field Chickweed, *C. arvense*
  (*C. strictum*), bracts with thin, translucent
  edges, all states; **American Starwort,**
  Stellaria americana, wide, grayish leaves, MT.

all white

►NOT glandular hairy,
  Alpine Starwort
  Stellaria longipes
  (petals longer than sepals, leaves green)
  Altai Starwort, *S. irrigua*, plant purplish,
  petals shorter than sepals with lobes narrowly
  linear, CO, NM; *S. umbellata*, see page 58.

  Widespread but uncommon above treeline:
  Northern Starwort, *S. calycantha*, flat eggshaped
  leaves, all states; **Stitchwort,** *S. longifolia*, minute bumps
  (tubercles) on leaf margins, floral bracts not green, all states.

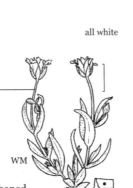

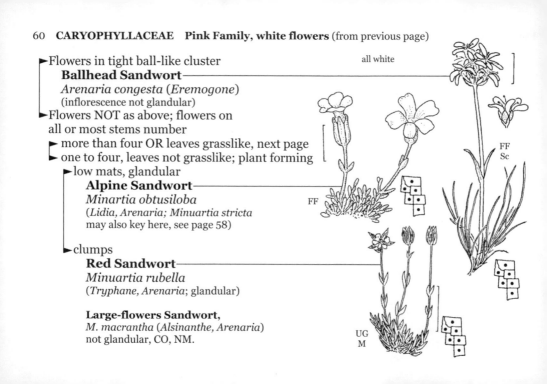

►Flowers in tight ball-like cluster   all white
  Ballhead Sandwort————————————————————————————
  Arenaria congesta (*Eremogone*)
  (inflorescence not glandular)
►Flowers NOT as above; flowers on
all or most stems number
  ► more than four OR leaves grasslike, next page
  ► one to four, leaves not grasslike; plant forming
    ►low mats, glandular
      Alpine Sandwort————
      Minartia obtusiloba   FF
      (*Lidia, Arenaria; Minuartia stricta*
      may also key here, see page 58)

    ►clumps
      Red Sandwort————————————————
      Minuartia rubella
      (*Tryphane, Arenaria*; glandular)

      Large-flowers Sandwort,
      M. macrantha (*Alsinanthe, Arenaria*)
      not glandular, CO, NM.

FF
Sc

UG
M

►Leaves under 15mm long,
needle-like
　Nuttall's Sandwort————
　Minuartia nuttallii
　(*Minuopsis, Arenaria*)
　(flowering stems short, leafy, glandular
　hairy, likes gravelly unstable slopes)

　Prickly Sandwort, *Arenaria aculeata*
　(*Eremogone*), low prickly mats with
　tall, nearly naked flower stems,
　ID, MT, NM, UT.

►Leaves longer, grass-like
　Fendler's Sandwort————
　Arenaria fendleri
　(*Eremogone*)
　(not forming prickly mats,
　inflorescence glandular)

all white

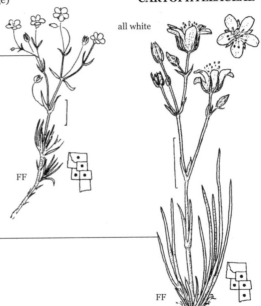

FF

STONECROP FAMILY(*Crassulaceae*)
Succulent herbs, flowers with four or five
separate, pointed petals, and four or five
pistils which are slightly united at base.

►Flowers pink, in rounded cluster
  Rosecrown——
    Sedum rhodanthum
    (*Clementsia rhodantha*)

►Flowers crimson, in more or less
  flat-topped cluster
  Kingscrown——
    Sedum integrifolium
      (*Rhodiola integrifolia, S. rosea*)

►Flowers yellow (may have reddish tinge)
  Common Stonecrop——
    Sedum lanceolatum
    (*Amerosedum*)
  Weakstem Stonecrop, *S. debile*,
  opposite stem leaves, ID, UT, WY.

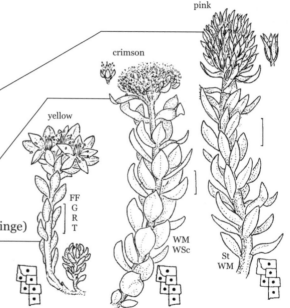

pink

crimson

yellow

FF
G
R
T

WM
WSc

St
WM

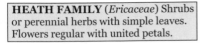

HEATH FAMILY (*Ericaceae*) Shrubs or perennial herbs with simple leaves. Flowers regular with united petals.

▶Leaves NOT needle or scale-like, next page
▶Leaves flat, needle-like, with edges rolled under, densely covering stem; flowers
　▶dingy white or greenish
　　Yellow Mountain Heath—————————
　　Phyllodoce glanduliflora
　▶pink
　　Pink Mountain Heath—————
　　Phyllodoce empetriformis

　　Hybrid Mountain Heath,
　　Phyllodoce X intermedia, hybrid between
　　P. glanduliflora and *P. empetriformis*,
　　ID, MT, WY.

▶Leaves narrow, tiny, scale-like, overlapping in four vertical rows
　　White Mountain Heather————————
　　Cassiope mertensiana

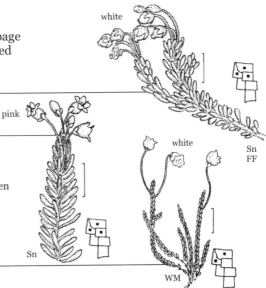

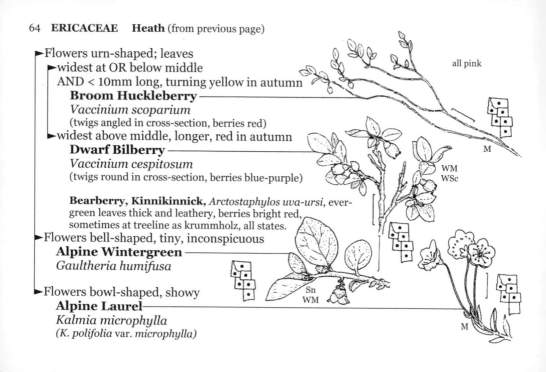

▶Flowers urn-shaped; leaves
  ▶widest at OR below middle
  AND < 10mm long, turning yellow in autumn
    Broom Huckleberry
    Vaccinium scoparium
    (twigs angled in cross-section, berries red)
  ▶widest above middle, longer, red in autumn
    Dwarf Bilberry
    Vaccinium cespitosum
    (twigs round in cross-section, berries blue-purple)

    Bearberry, Kinnikinnick, *Arctostaphylos uva-ursi,* ever-
    green leaves thick and leathery, berries bright red,
    sometimes at treeline as krummholz, all states.
▶Flowers bell-shaped, tiny, inconspicuous
    Alpine Wintergreen
    Gaultheria humifusa

▶Flowers bowl-shaped, showy
    Alpine Laurel
    Kalmia microphylla
    (*K. polifolia* var. *microphylla*)

all pink

M

WM
WSc

Sn
WM

M

PEA FAMILY (*Fabaceae* or *Leguminosae*)
Flowers irregular, pea-shaped. Leaves alternate
and compound. Fruits pea or bean-like.

►Leaflets > three (at least some), page 67

►Leaflets three; flowers

►all erect or ascending, next page

►nodding (at least some); plant

►growing in Colorado
or New Mexico
Brandegee's Clover
Trifolium brandegeei

►growing in Idaho, Montana
or Wyoming
Hayden's Clover
Trifolium haydenii

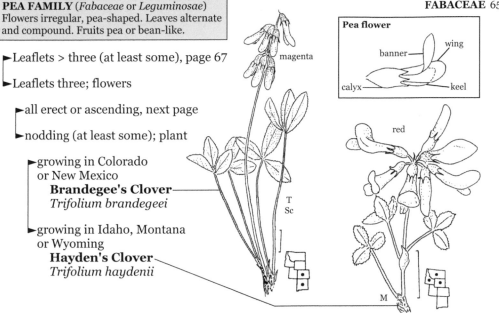

Pea flower — banner, wing, calyx, keel

magenta

red

T Sc

M

►Flowers one to three per stem
    Dwarf Clover————————————————————————
    Trifolium nanum

pink

FF
M

►Flowers > three per stem; corolla
  ►somewhat uniformly colored, deep or bright rose
    Parry's Clover————————————
    Trifolium parryi
    (*T. salictorum*)
    (leaflets elliptical, often toothed, mostly
    hairless, bracts obvious, some united)

pink-magenta

pink and white
bicolor

    T. attenuatum, leaflet length > 4x width,
    flowers pale pink and some nodding,
    otherwise like *T. dasyphyllum* but
    larger, sCO, nNM; *T. brandeegei,*
    leaflet length < 4x width, flowers
    deep magenta, pendant, sCO, nNM.

Sn
WM

  ►bicolored with light banner and
  wings AND darker pink or purple keel
    Alpine Clover————————————————————————
    Trifolium dasyphyllum
    (leaflets narrow often folded, grayish, bracts tiny or absent, not united)

FF

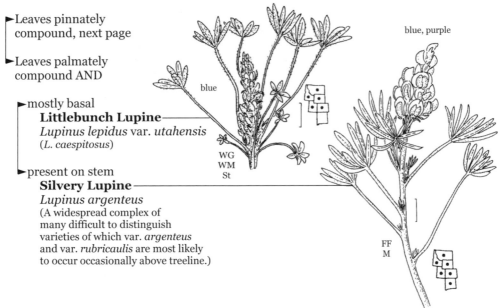

►Leaves pinnately
compound, next page

►Leaves palmately
compound AND

    ►mostly basal
    Littlebunch Lupine
    Lupinus lepidus var. *utahensis*
    (*L. caespitosus*)

    ►present on stem
    Silvery Lupine
    Lupinus argenteus
    (A widespread complex of
    many difficult to distinguish
    varieties of which var. *argenteus*
    and var. *rubricaulis* are most likely
    to occur occasionally above treeline.)

blue

blue, purple

WG
WM
St

FF
M

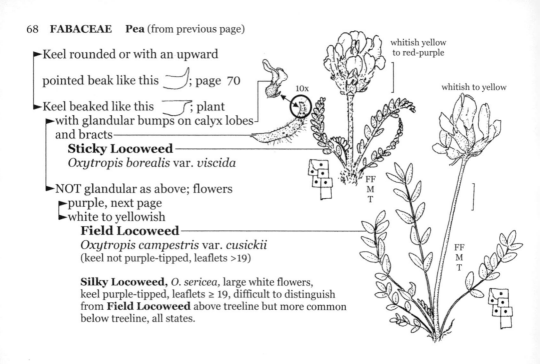

►Keel rounded or with an upward

pointed beak like this ⌐ʃ; page 70

►Keel beaked like this ⌐ʃ; plant
  ►with glandular bumps on calyx lobes
  and bracts
    Sticky Locoweed
    Oxytropis borealis var. *viscida*

►NOT glandular as above; flowers
  ►purple, next page
  ►white to yellowish
    Field Locoweed
    Oxytropis campestris var. *cusickii*
    (keel not purple-tipped, leaflets >19)

Silky Locoweed, *O. sericea,* large white flowers,
keel purple-tipped, leaflets ≥ 19, difficult to distinguish
from **Field Locoweed** above treeline but more common
below treeline, all states.

whitish yellow
to red-purple

10x

whitish to yellow

FF
M
T

FF
M
T

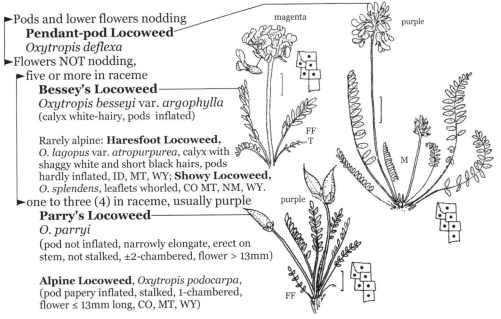

►Pods and lower flowers nodding
  Pendant-pod Locoweed
  Oxytropis deflexa
►Flowers NOT nodding,
  ►five or more in raceme
    Bessey's Locoweed
    Oxytropis besseyi var. *argophylla*
    (calyx white-hairy, pods inflated)

    Rarely alpine: **Haresfoot Locoweed,**
    O. lagopus var. *atropurpurea,* calyx with
    shaggy white and short black hairs, pods
    hardly inflated, ID, MT, WY; **Showy Locoweed,**
    O. splendens, leaflets whorled, CO MT, NM, WY.

  ►one to three (4) in raceme, usually purple
    Parry's Locoweed
    O. parryi
    (pod not inflated, narrowly elongate, erect on
    stem, not stalked, ±2-chambered, flower > 13mm)

    Alpine Locoweed, *Oxytropis podocarpa*,
    (pod papery inflated, stalked, 1-chambered,
    flower ≤ 13mm long, CO, MT, WY)

magenta   purple

purple

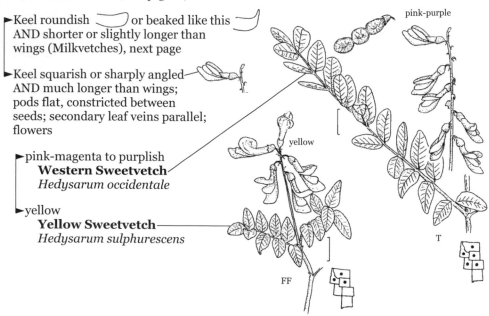

►Keel roundish ⌣ or beaked like this ⌣
AND shorter or slightly longer than
wings (Milkvetches), next page

►Keel squarish or sharply angled
AND much longer than wings;
pods flat, constricted between
seeds; secondary leaf veins parallel;
flowers

pink-purple

  ►pink-magenta to purplish
    Western Sweetvetch
    Hedysarum occidentale

  ►yellow
    Yellow Sweetvetch
    Hedysarum sulphurescens

yellow

FF

T

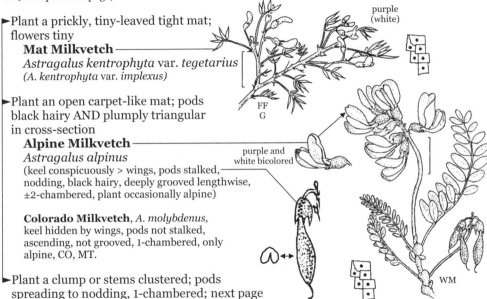

►Plant a prickly, tiny-leaved tight mat;
flowers tiny
   Mat Milkvetch
   Astragalus kentrophyta var. *tegetarius*
   (A. kentrophyta var. *implexus)*

purple
(white)

FF
G

►Plant an open carpet-like mat; pods
black hairy AND plumply triangular
in cross-section
   Alpine Milkvetch
   Astragalus alpinus
   (keel conspicuously > wings, pods stalked,
   nodding, black hairy, deeply grooved lengthwise,
   ±2-chambered, plant occasionally alpine)

purple and
white bicolored

   Colorado Milkvetch, *A. molybdenus,*
   keel hidden by wings, pods not stalked,
   ascending, not grooved, 1-chambered, only
   alpine, CO, MT.

►Plant a clump or stems clustered; pods
spreading to nodding, 1-chambered; next page

WM

►Wing notched at tip
Indian Milkvetch
Astragalus australis var. *glabriusculus*
(keel hidden by wings, pod stalked,
somewhat flattened)

►Wing rounded at tip
Western Milkvetch
Astragalus robbinsii var. *minor*
(keel hidden by wings, pod stalked,
black and white hairy, plumply
triangular in cross-section)

Weedy Milkvetch, *A. miser* var. *tenuifolius*,
keel ≥ wings, pods not stalked, flattened,
leaflets inrolled and appearing linear,
pick-ax hairs, ID, MT, WY; others
difficult to separate.

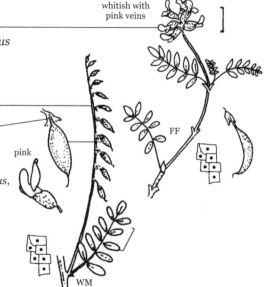

whitish with
pink veins

pink

FF

WM

GENTIAN FAMILY (*Gentianaceae*)
Herbs with simple, entire leaves which
are opposite or whorled on stem.
Flowers regular, petals four or five.

►Petals clearly united, next page

►Petals appear separate; flowers

►greenish white
Monument Plant, Elkweed
Frasera speciosa
(*Swertia radiata*)

►dull purple or blue
Star Gentian
Swertia perennis

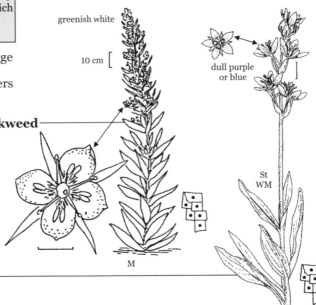

greenish white

10 cm

dull purple
or blue

St
WM

M

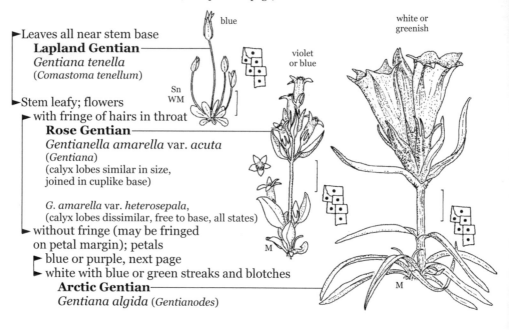

blue

white or
greenish

violet
or blue

►Leaves all near stem base
　Lapland Gentian
　Gentiana tenella
　(*Comastoma tenellum*)

Sn
WM

►Stem leafy; flowers
　► with fringe of hairs in throat
　　Rose Gentian
　　Gentianella amarella var. *acuta*
　　(*Gentiana*)
　　(calyx lobes similar in size,
　　joined in cuplike base)

　　G. amarella var. *heterosepala*,
　　(calyx lobes dissimilar, free to base, all states)

　► without fringe (may be fringed
　　on petal margin); petals
　　► blue or purple, next page
　　► white with blue or green streaks and blotches
　　　Arctic Gentian
　　　Gentiana algida (*Gentianodes*)

M

M

► Corolla four-lobed, without
secondary lobes, next page

► Corolla four- or five-lobed with
alternating secondary lobes; plant

► tiny, usually four-lobed
Moss Gentian———
Gentiana prostrata
(*Ciminalis, Chondrophylla*)

► large, five-lobed
Parry Gentian———
Gentiana parryi
(*Pneumonanthe*)
(minutely hairy leaf margins,
leaf length > 2x width)

Explorer's Gentian, *G. calycosa,* not hairy,
leaf length < 2x width, ID, MT, UT, WY.

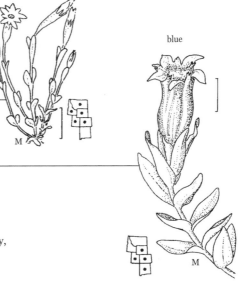

►Corolla lobes fringed on
margins; flowers
  ►fragrant, with two bract-like
  leaves immediately under flowers
    Fragrant Gentian—
    Gentianopsis barbellata

  ►NOT fragrant, without bract-like
  leaves immediately under flowers
    Rocky Mountain Fringed Gentian—
    Gentianopsis detonsa var. *elegans*
    (*G. thermalis*)

►Corolla lobes NOT fringed on margins
    Four-parted Gentian—
    Gentianella propinqua
    (*Gentiana*)

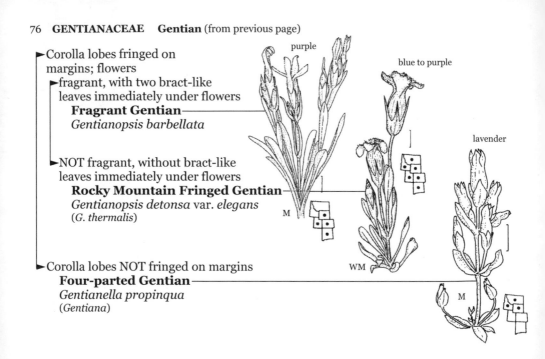

purple

blue to purple

lavender

CURRANT FAMILY (*Grossulariaceae*) Shrubs with palmately lobed leaves. Flowers with five small petals and five sepals. Calyx may be tubular or saucer-shaped and may be colored. Plant may be spiny.

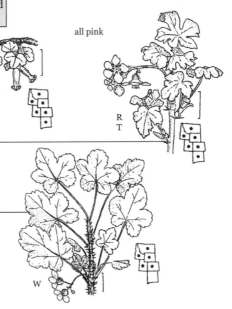

all pink

►Stems not spiny; berry black
  Squaw Currant
  Ribes cereum

►Stems spiny; leaves
  ► deeply cleft > ¾ of way to base, glandular hairy; berries red; flowers saucer-shaped
    Alpine Prickly Currant
    Ribes montigenum

  ► cleft < 2/3 of way to base, NOT glandular hairy; berries purple
    Swamp Black Currant
    Ribes lacustre
    (flowers cup-shaped; usually below treeline)

    Henderson's Gooseberry, *R. hendersonii,*
    flowers trumpet-shaped, plant gnarly with
    very spiny leaf nodes, cID, wMT.

WATERLEAF FAMILY (*Hydrophyllaceae*)
Coiled clusters of five united-petaled, regular flowers with five stamens often extending beyond the petals. Ovary superior.

▶Leaves entire (all or most)
Whiteleaf Phacelia
Phacelia hastata

▶Leaves deeply divided OR lobed nearly to midvein
Silky Phacelia
Phacelia sericea
(inflorescence length > width)

▶Leaves coarsely toothed OR lobed less than 2/3 of the way to the midvein
Lyall's Phacelia
Phacelia lyallii
(inflorescence length < width)

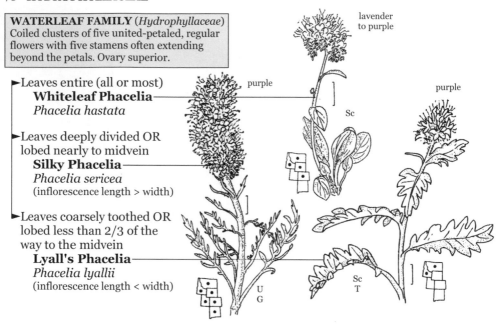

lavender to purple

purple

purple

Sc

U G

Sc T

LILY FAMILY *(Liliaceae)* Regular flowers with three petals, three usually petal-like sepals, six stamens, superior ovary.

yellow

►Petals bright yellow AND
usually curved backward
   Avalanche Lily———
   Erythronium grandiflorum

white

►Petals various colors but not bright yellow AND usually not curved backward (except Western Stenanthium); flowers

   ► one (rarely two) per stem
      Alp Lily———
      Lloydia serotina

   ► several per stem, AND
      ►in an elongate open raceme or panicle, next page

      ►bunched in a ball, spike or umbel, page 81

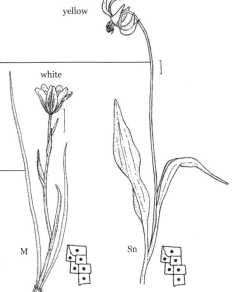

M   Sn

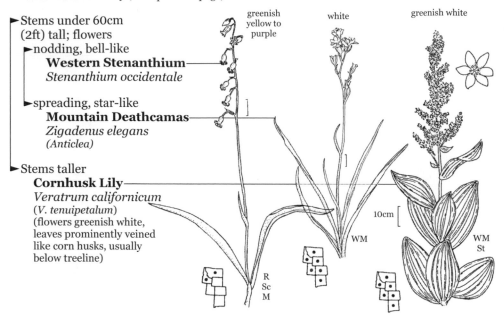

greenish yellow to purple

white

greenish white

►Stems under 60cm
(2ft) tall; flowers
►nodding, bell-like
  Western Stenanthium———
  Stenanthium occidentale

►spreading, star-like
  Mountain Deathcamas———
  Zigadenus elegans
  (Anticlea)

►Stems taller
  Cornhusk Lily———
  Veratrum californicum
  (V. tenuipetalum)
  (flowers greenish white,
  leaves prominently veined
  like corn husks, usually
  below treeline)

10cm

WM
St

WM

R
Sc
M

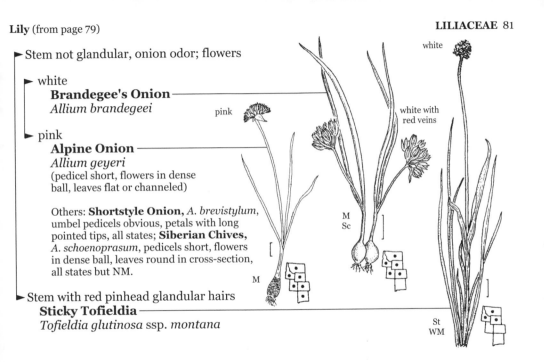

► Stem not glandular, onion odor; flowers

  ► white
    Brandegee's Onion
    Allium brandegeei

  ► pink
    Alpine Onion
    Allium geyeri
    (pedicel short, flowers in dense
    ball, leaves flat or channeled)

    Others: **Shortstyle Onion,** *A. brevistylum*,
    umbel pedicels obvious, petals with long
    pointed tips, all states; **Siberian Chives,**
    A. schoenoprasum, pedicels short, flowers
    in dense ball, leaves round in cross-section,
    all states but NM.

► Stem with red pinhead glandular hairs
  Sticky Tofieldia
  Tofieldia glutinosa ssp. *montana*

pink

white

white with
red veins

M
Sc

M

St
WM

FLAX FAMILY (*Linaceae*) Flowers regular with five separate petals and sepals, five stamens, superior ovary. Petals fall easily. Leaves alternate, narrow.

Blue Flax
Linum lewisii
(*Adenolinum*)

EVENING PRIMROSE FAMILY (*Onagraceae*)
Flowers regular with four separate petals (floral tube may be present), four sepals, eight stamens, inferior ovary.

► Flowers more than 13mm wide, next page
► Flowers smaller,
  ► nodding in bud; plants in dense clumps ≤ 20cm (8 in) with spreading, curvy stems

Alpine Willowherb
Epilobium anagallidifolium
(*E. alpinum*)

► erect in bud

various Willowherbs
*E. clavatum, E. halleanum, E. hornemannii,
E. lactiflorum, E. saximontanum* and many other widespread species difficult to separate.

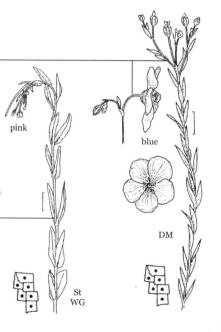

pink

blue

DM

St
WG

Evening Primrose (from previous page)

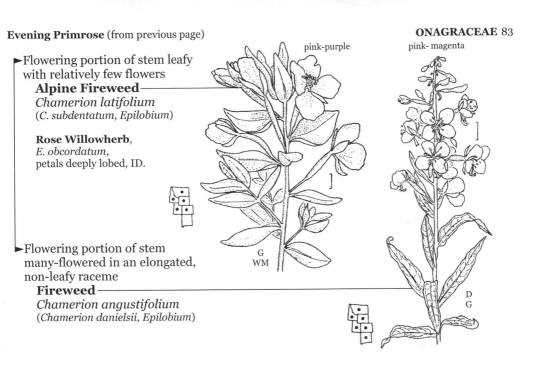

pink-purple

pink- magenta

►Flowering portion of stem leafy
with relatively few flowers
  Alpine Fireweed
  Chamerion latifolium
  (*C. subdentatum, Epilobium*)

  Rose Willowherb,
  E. obcordatum,
  petals deeply lobed, ID.

►Flowering portion of stem
many-flowered in an elongated,
non-leafy raceme
  Fireweed
  Chamerion angustifolium
  (*Chamerion danielsii, Epilobium*)

G
WM

D
G

POPPY FAMILY (*Papaveraceae*)
Flowers regular with four to six separate
petals. Sepals two or three, falling early.
Stamens many, ovary superior.

yellow
to whitish

►Flowers pale yellow or white;
petals ≥ 10cm
Alpine Poppy——————
Papaver radicatum ssp. *kluanense*
(*P. kluanense*)

orange to
pinkish orange

►Flowers orange to pinkish orange;
petals ≤ 10cm
Dwarf Alpine Poppy——
Papaver pygmaeum

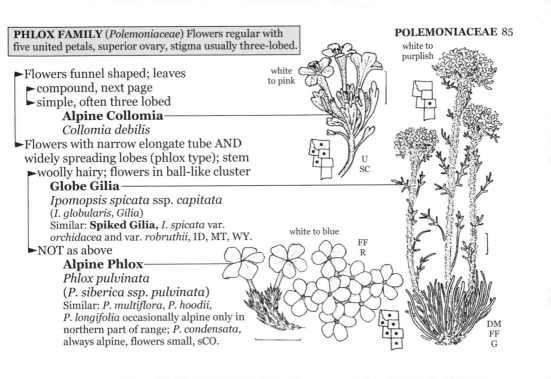

PHLOX FAMILY (*Polemoniaceae*) Flowers regular with five united petals, superior ovary, stigma usually three-lobed.

white to pink

white to purplish

►Flowers funnel shaped; leaves
►compound, next page
►simple, often three lobed
Alpine Collomia
Collomia debilis

►Flowers with narrow elongate tube AND widely spreading lobes (phlox type); stem
►woolly hairy; flowers in ball-like cluster
Globe Gilia
Ipomopsis spicata ssp. *capitata*
(*I. globularis*, Gilia)
Similar: **Spiked Gilia**, *I. spicata* var. *orchidacea* and var. *robruthii*, ID, MT, WY.

►NOT as above
Alpine Phlox
Phlox pulvinata
(*P. siberica ssp. pulvinata*)
Similar: *P. multiflora*, *P. hoodii*, *P. longifolia* occasionally alpine only in northern part of range; *P. condensata*, always alpine, flowers small, sCO.

white to blue

U
SC

FF
R

DM
FF
G

►Leaflets appear whorled
Sky Pilot
Polemonium viscosum
(skunky odor, purple flowers not widely flaring,
tube ≤ 10mm wide at mouth, inflorescence
fan-shaped, common on stable tundra)
Gray's Peak Sky Pilot, *P. confertum*,
light blue widely flaring flowers, tube
mouth ≥10mm, inflorescence globe-shaped,
unstable talus and scree, CO;
Honey Sky Pilot, *P. brandegeei* ,
cream-yellow flowers, CO, NM, UT, WY.

►Leaflets NOT whorled
Subalpine Jacobs Ladder
Polemonium pulcherrimum
var. *delicatum*

Showy Jacob's Ladder, *P. pulcherrimum*
var. *pulcherrimum*, similar but with many
basal leaves in tufts, ID, MT, UT, WY.

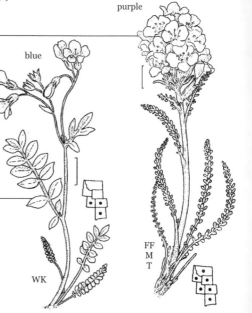

purple

blue

WK

FF
M
T

BUCKWHEAT FAMILY (*Polygonaceae*)
Flowers regular with four, five or six petal-like segments. Stipules sheathing (except in *Eriogonum*).

►Flowers yellow, page 90
►Flowers white/cream to rose/red; plant
  ►loosely matted; leaves hairy OR not, page 89
  ►single- or few-stemmed; leaf blade
    ►much longer than wide, next page
    ►heart or kidney shaped
      Alpine Sorrel
      Oxyria digyna
  ►tightly matted; leaves woolly at least below; corolla
    ►NOT hairy
      Cushion Buckwheat
      Eriogonum ovalifolium var. *depressum*
    ►hairy externally; leaf margin rolled under
      Matted Buckwheat
      Eriogonum caespitosum
      (usually bright yellow, rarely above treeline)

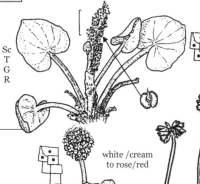

pink

Sc T G R

white /cream to rose/red

FF

FF

►Bulblets present on spike
below flowering portion
Alpine Bistort
Polygonum viviparum
(*Bistorta vivipara*)

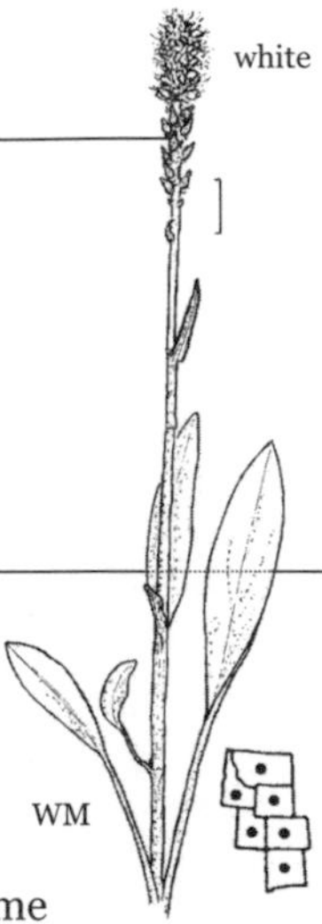

white

reddish

white
pink in
bud

►Bulblets absent; flowers in
►loose panicle
Mountain Sorrel
Rumex paucifolius
(*Acetosella*)

►dense cotton-ball-like raceme
American Bistort
Polygonum bistortoides
(*Bistorta*)

WM

U
M

FF
M

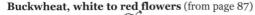

►Corolla hairy→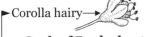

white

Oarleaf Buckwheat
Eriogonum pyrolifolium
var. *coryphaeum*
(leaves not hairy)

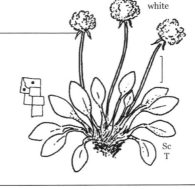

Sc
T

►Corolla NOT hairy
Subalpine Buckwheat
Eriogonum umbellatum var. *majus*
(*Eriogonum subalpinum*)
(leaf blade oval, not hairy,
occasional above treeline)

Colorado Buckwheat, *E. coloradense*,
leaf blade much longer than wide,
lower surface hairy, CO.

FF
DM

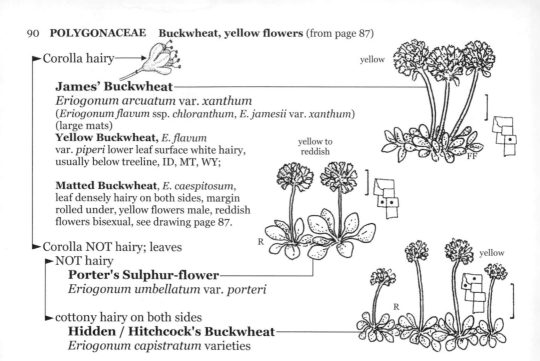

►Corolla hairy——

yellow

James' Buckwheat——
Eriogonum arcuatum var. *xanthum*
(*Eriogonum flavum* ssp. *chloranthum*, *E. jamesii* var. *xanthum*)
(large mats)
Yellow Buckwheat, *E. flavum*
var. *piperi* lower leaf surface white hairy,
usually below treeline, ID, MT, WY;

yellow to
reddish

Matted Buckwheat, *E. caespitosum*,
leaf densely hairy on both sides, margin
rolled under, yellow flowers male, reddish
flowers bisexual, see drawing page 87.

►Corolla NOT hairy; leaves
  ►NOT hairy
    Porter's Sulphur-flower——
    Eriogonum umbellatum var. *porteri*

yellow

►cottony hairy on both sides
  Hidden / Hitchcock's Buckwheat——
  Eriogonum capistratum varieties

PURSLANE FAMILY (*Portulacaceae*)
Flowers regular with four to eight petals, which are separate or slightly united at base, two sepals. Ovary superior, stamens opposite petals. Leaves simple.

►Flowers in ball-like cluster, petals four
Pussypaws
Calyptridium umbellatum
var. *caudicifera*
(*Spraguea umbellata*)

►Flowers solitary OR in open cluster, petals five to eight; leaves

►more than two, next page

►two, opposite
Lanceleaf Spring Beauty
Claytonia lanceolata

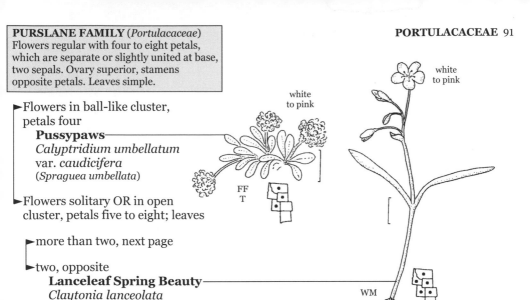

white to pink

white to pink

FF
T

WM

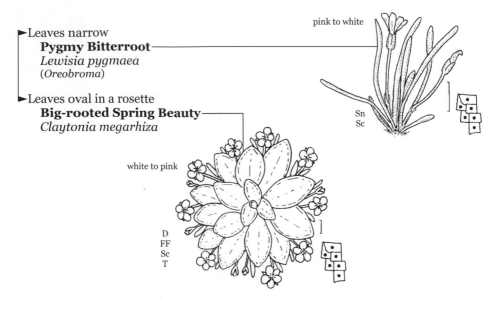

pink to white

►Leaves narrow
   Pygmy Bitterroot
   Lewisia pygmaea
   (*Oreobroma*)

►Leaves oval in a rosette
   Big-rooted Spring Beauty
   Claytonia megarhiza

Sn
Sc

white to pink

D
FF
Sc
T

PRIMROSE FAMILY (*Primulaceae*)
Flowers regular with five united petals,
ovary superior. Stamens opposite petals.
Leaves simple, mostly basal.

► Flowers white AND
  ► tiny (less than 4mm wide); plant
    not mat-forming
    Rock Primrose
    Androsace septentrionalis

  ► larger, fragrant; plant mat-forming
    Rockjasmine
    Androsace chamaejasme
    ssp. *carinata*
    (*A. chamaejasme* ssp. *lehmanniana*)

► Flowers pink; plant
  ► mat-forming; petals entire
    Rocky Mountain Douglasia
    Douglasia montana

  ► NOT matted; petals notched OR
    swept back, next page

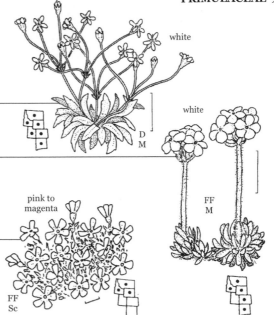

white

white

pink to
magenta

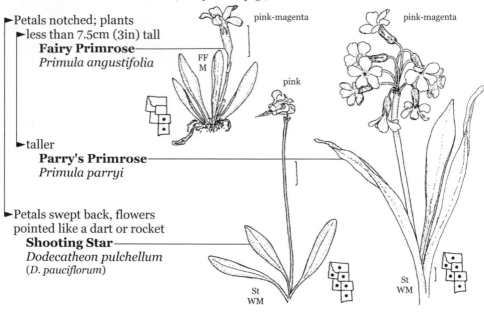

►Petals notched; plants
►less than 7.5cm (3in) tall
   Fairy Primrose
   Primula angustifolia

pink-magenta

pink-magenta

FF
M

pink

►taller
   Parry's Primrose
   Primula parryi

►Petals swept back, flowers
pointed like a dart or rocket
   Shooting Star
   Dodecatheon pulchellum
   (*D. pauciflorum*)

St
WM

St
WM

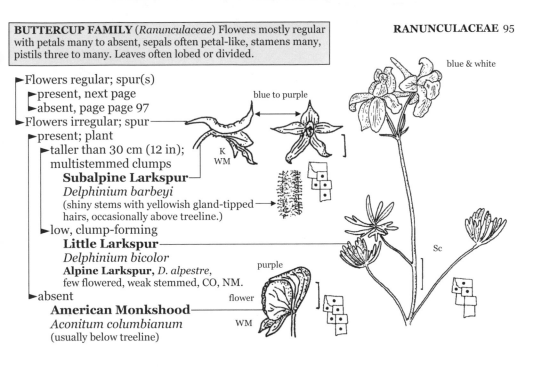

BUTTERCUP FAMILY (*Ranunculaceae*) Flowers mostly regular with petals many to absent, sepals often petal-like, stamens many, pistils three to many. Leaves often lobed or divided.

blue & white

►Flowers regular; spur(s)
  ►present, next page
  ►absent, page page 97

►Flowers irregular; spur
  ►present; plant

blue to purple

  ►taller than 30 cm (12 in);
    multistemmed clumps
      Subalpine Larkspur
      Delphinium barbeyi
      (shiny stems with yellowish gland-tipped
      hairs, occasionally above treeline.)

K
WM

  ►low, clump-forming
      Little Larkspur
      Delphinium bicolor
      Alpine Larkspur, *D. alpestre*,
      few flowered, weak stemmed, CO, NM.

Sc

purple

►absent
    American Monkshood
    Aconitum columbianum
    (usually below treeline)

flower

WM

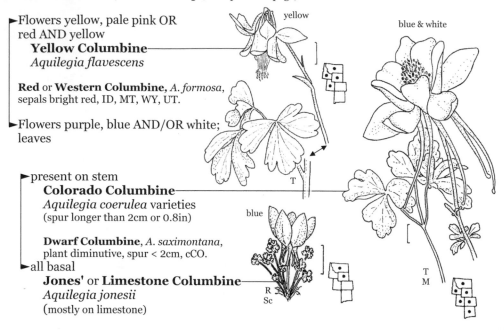

►Flowers yellow, pale pink OR
red AND yellow
   Yellow Columbine
   Aquilegia flavescens

Red or **Western Columbine**, *A. formosa*,
sepals bright red, ID, MT, WY, UT.

►Flowers purple, blue AND/OR white;
leaves

►present on stem
   Colorado Columbine
   Aquilegia coerulea varieties
   (spur longer than 2cm or 0.8in)

   Dwarf Columbine, *A. saximontana*,
   plant diminutive, spur < 2cm, cCO.

►all basal
   Jones' or **Limestone Columbine**
   Aquilegia jonesii
   (mostly on limestone)

yellow

blue & white

blue

Buttercup, flowers regular, no spur (from page 95) **RANUNCULACEAE** 97

►Petals NOT bright yellow AND NOT shiny, page 99

►Petals bright yellow with shiny upper surface (Buttercups); basal leaves

all yellow

►finely divided into thread-like segments
Snow or **Alpine Buttercup**
Ranunculus adoneus

Sn

►simple and entire
Waterplantain Buttercup
Ranunculus alismifolius
var. *montanus*

►simple and lobed, next page

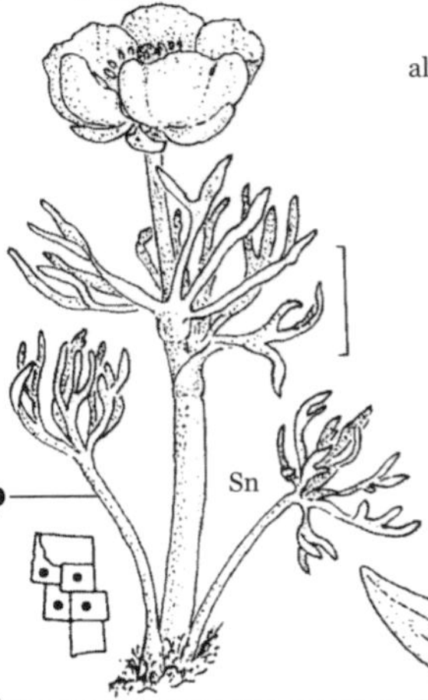

WM

►Fruits NOT hairy
Alpine Buttercup————————————————
Ranunculus eschscholtzii and varieties
(most leaves deeply lobed, petals > 0.5mm,
style straight or slightly curved)

Rocky Mt. Buttercup, *R. macauleyi*,
stems and sepals black hairy, stem leaves
with slightly toothed tips, CO, NM;

►Fruits hairy
Drab Buttercup————————
Ranunculus inamoenus
(basal leaves toothed to shallowly
lobed, petals < 0.5mm, style hooked)

Birdfoot or **Surefoot Buttercup**,
R. pedatifidus, basal leaves deeply cleft
to base, fruits hairy, CO, MT, NM, UT, WY;
Pygmy Buttercup, *R. pygmaeus*,
plant less than 5cm (2in) tall,
CO, ID, MT, UT, WY.

all yellow

fruit

WM

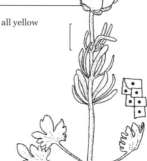

WM

Buttercup, not yellow (from page 97)

▶Flowers small AND inconspicuous
  Alpine Meadowrue
  Thalictrum alpinum

greenish
to purple

white

WM

▶Flowers conspicuous, showy; plant
  ▶ entirely hairless, page 101
  ▶ hairy on stem and/or leaves; flowers
    ▶ NOT large and crocus-like, next page

bluish

    ▶ large and crocus-like; styles elongate
      and feathery at maturity; petals

    ▶blue, purple or lavender
      American Pasqueflower
      Cutleaf Anemone
      Pulsatilla patens ssp. *multifida*
      (*Anemone ludoviciana*)

Sn
M

    ▶white to cream
      Western Pasqueflower
      Pulsatilla occidentalis (*Anemone*)

fuzzy
fruit

M

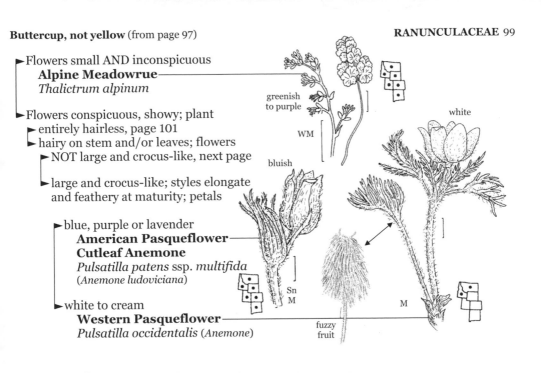

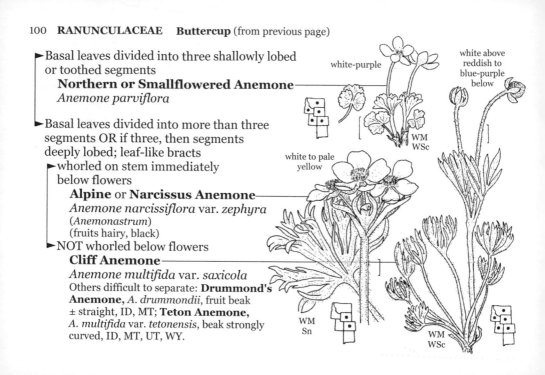

►Basal leaves divided into three shallowly lobed or toothed segments
Northern or Smallflowered Anemone
Anemone parviflora

white-purple

white above reddish to blue-purple below

►Basal leaves divided into more than three segments OR if three, then segments deeply lobed; leaf-like bracts
►whorled on stem immediately below flowers
Alpine or **Narcissus Anemone**
Anemone narcissiflora var. *zephyra*
(*Anemonastrum*)
(fruits hairy, black)

white to pale yellow

►NOT whorled below flowers
Cliff Anemone
Anemone multifida var. *saxicola*
Others difficult to separate: **Drummond's Anemone**, *A. drummondii*, fruit beak ± straight, ID, MT; **Teton Anemone**, *A. multifida* var. *tetonensis*, beak strongly curved, ID, MT, UT, WY.

WM
WSc

WM
Sn

WM
WSc

►Leaves entire or shallowly scalloped
 Marsh Marigold
 Caltha leptosepala
 (*Psychrophila, C. biflora*)
 (often carpeting wet snowmelt areas)

►Leaves palmately cleft into lobes
 Globeflower
 Trollius albiflorus
 (*T. laxus* var. *albiflorus*)
 (fruits not hairy, dark brown)

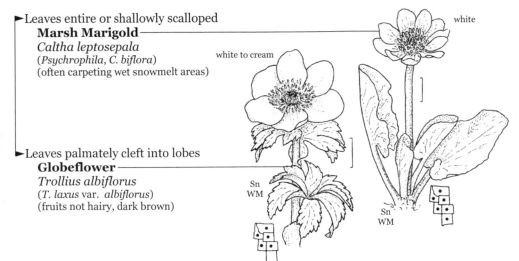

white

white to cream

Sn
WM

Sn
WM

ROSE FAMILY (*Rosaceae*) Flowers regular with five separate petals, five sepals which appear united at base and may appear to be ten due to the presence of small bracts, usually many stamens. Petals, sepals and stamens set on the rim of a floral cup. Leaves usually with stipules.

►Flowers yellow, page 105

►Flowers white or pink; leaves
  ►compound, page 104

  ►simple; flowers
    ►one per stem, next page
    ►many per stem, AND
      ►pink to red; shrub
        Pink Spiraea, Meadowsweet
        Spiraea splendens
        (*S. densiflora*)

    ►white; mat plant
      Rockmat
      Petrophyton caespitosum

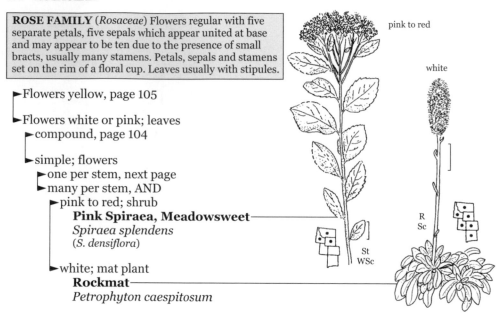

pink to red

white

St
WSc

R
Sc

►Petals number eight
Alpine Dryad————
Dryas octopetala ssp. *hookeriana*
(pioneer plant forming large mats on
scree, leaf undersurface densely woolly,
filaments not hairy, common and widespread)

white

FF
Sc
D

►Petals number five
Kelseya————
Kelseya uniflora
(dense tiny leaved mats hang in
crevices and perch on limestone, rare)

pink

R

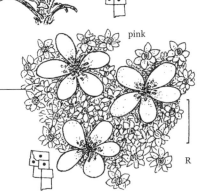

►Flowers reddish-pink
  Pink Plumes
  Geum triflorum
  (Erythrocoma triflora)
  (alpine only in northern
  part of range)

►Flowers white; plant a
  ►prickly-stemmed shrub
    Raspberry
    Rubus idaeus
    ssp. *melanolasius*
    (*R. idaeus* var. *strigosus*)

  ►low herb with runners
    Wild Strawberry
    Fragaria virginiana
    ssp. *glauca*

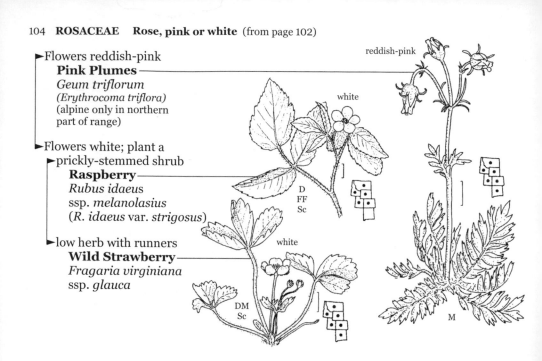

reddish-pink

white

D
FF
Sc

white

DM
Sc

M

►Leaves simple
　Yellow Dryad
　Dryas drummondii
　(filaments hairy at base,
　rocky wet areas)

►Leaves compound; plant

　►NOT a shrub, next page

　►a shrub
　　Shrubby Potentilla
　　Pentaphylloides floribunda
　　(*Potentilla fruticosa*,
　　Pentaphylloides fruticosa)

both yellow

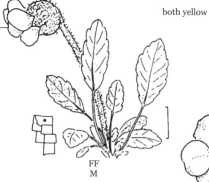

FF
M

St
WM

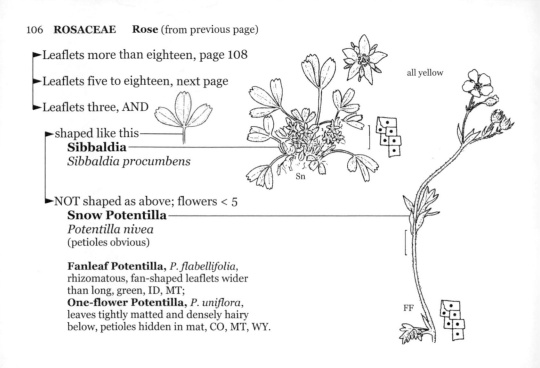

►Leaflets more than eighteen, page 108

►Leaflets five to eighteen, next page

►Leaflets three, AND

►shaped like this ——
Sibbaldia ——
Sibbaldia procumbens

all yellow

Sn

►NOT shaped as above; flowers < 5
Snow Potentilla ——
Potentilla nivea
(petioles obvious)

Fanleaf Potentilla, *P. flabellifolia*,
rhizomatous, fan-shaped leaflets wider
than long, green, ID, MT;
One-flower Potentilla, *P. uniflora*,
leaves tightly matted and densely hairy
below, petioles hidden in mat, CO, MT, WY.

FF

►Leaflets five to nine, AND
  ►densely white-hairy below
    Early Potentilla
    Potentilla concinna
    (leaflets 5, palmately arranged,
    toothed only above middle)

    Colorado Cinquefoil, *P. subjuga*, 3 leaflets
    palmately arranged with 2 or 4 leaflets
    below, style > 1.2mm long, CO, NM;
    Red Stem Potentilla, *P. rubricaulis*,
    leaflets pinnately arranged, style < 1.2mm,
    CO, MT, neUT, WY.

  ►NOT densely hairy, green or bluish
    Varileaf Potentilla
    Potentilla diversifolia
    (leaflets usually five, palmate)

    Sticky Potentilla, *P. glandulosa* (*Drymocallis*),
    glandular, leaflets usually seven, pinnate, flowers
    pale yellow, CO, ID, MT, UT, WY.
►Leaflets nine to eighteen, narrow; next page

all yellow

FF

WM
FF

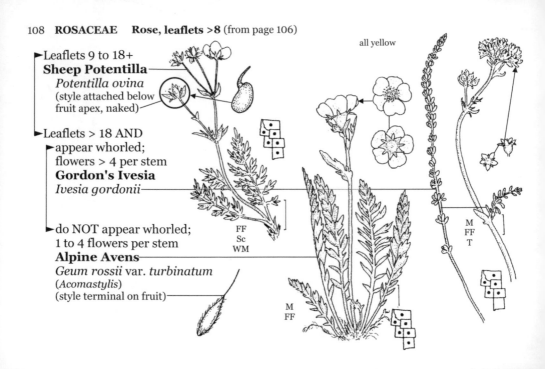

all yellow

►Leaflets 9 to 18+
Sheep Potentilla
Potentilla ovina
(style attached below
fruit apex, naked)

►Leaflets > 18 AND
►appear whorled;
flowers > 4 per stem
Gordon's Ivesia
Ivesia gordonii

►do NOT appear whorled;
1 to 4 flowers per stem
Alpine Avens
Geum rossii var. *turbinatum*
(*Acomastylis*)
(style terminal on fruit)

FF
Sc
WM

M
FF

M
FF
T

WILLOW FAMILY (*Salicaceae*) Shrubs with simple, entire or toothed, alternate leaves. Flowers catkins, calyx reduced or absent, petals absent. Fruit a capsule with many long-hairy seeds.

►Stems matted, creeping and rooting; most
  ►leaves rounded at apex, leathery; catkins
  terminating new growth
    Snow Willow————
    Salix reticulata var. *nana*
    (*S. reticulata* ssp. *saximontanus, S. nivalis*)
    Timberline Willow, *S. rotundifolia* ssp.
    dogdeana, leaf blades tiny ≤ 7mm, capsules
    not hairy, ID, MT, WY.

FF WM

all white to reddish in bud

  ►pointed at apex, NOT leathery; catkins on
  leafy, lateral branchlets
    Alpine Willow————
    Salix arctica var. *petraea*
    (*S. petrophila*)
    (leaf whitish beneath, veins prominent)
    Cascade Willow, *S. cascadensis*, leaf
    green beneath, veins obscure, all states but CO.

FF WM

►Stems erect or ascending,
forming low thickets, next page

► Leaves shiny dark green above;
year old branches shiny red;
catkin branchlets NOT leafy
   Planeleaf Willow———
   Salix planifolia
   (*S. phylicifolia*)

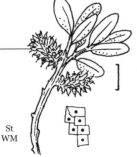

all white

St
WM

► Leaves sparsely hairy, dull and powdery
beneath; catkins on leafy branchlets
   Grey Willow———
   Salix glauca var. *villosa*
   (petiole 3-10mm long, yellowish)

St
WM

Shortfruit Willlow, *Salix brachycarpa*,
petiole 1-3mm, yellowish, usually not alpine; all states.

SAXIFRAGE FAMILY (Saxifragaceae) Flowers regular with five petals, five or ten stamens, one pistil commonly two-horned. Leaves often entirely basal and often palmately veined or lobed.

►Petals bright yellow, next page

►Petals white, greenish OR pale yellow (may have pink veins), page 113

►Petals purple to pink; leaves
  ►entire, tiny and opposite; a mat plant
    Purple Saxifrage
    Saxifraga oppositifolia

  ►deeply lobed or divided
    Woodland Star
    Lithophragma glabrum
    (see drawing page 113)

  ►twice shallowly lobed or toothed
    James' Saxifrage
    Telesonix jamesii
    (*Boykinia*)

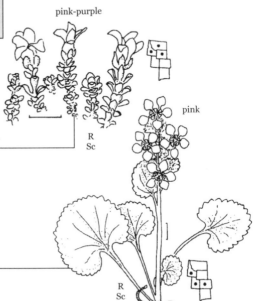

pink-purple

pink

R
Sc

R
Sc

►Stolons present
Whiplash Saxifrage
Saxifraga flagellaris
(*Hirculus platysepala* ssp. *crandallii*)
(propagates by runners, leaf
margins ciliate hairy)

all yellow

►Stolons absent
Goldbloom Saxifrage
Saxifraga chrysantha
(*Hirculus serpyllifolius* ssp. *chrysantha*)
(rosettes of tightly matted, fleshy,
hairless basal leaves,
petals orange-dotted near base)

Arctic Saxifrage, *S. hirculus*
(*Hirculus prorepens*), basal leaves
hairy, not or loosely matted, petals
sometimes dotted, wet areas, CO.

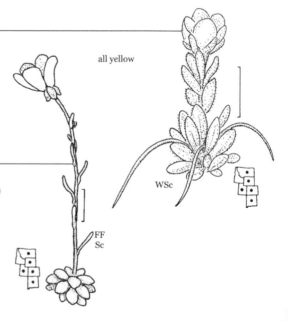

WSc

FF
Sc

Saxifrage (from page 111)

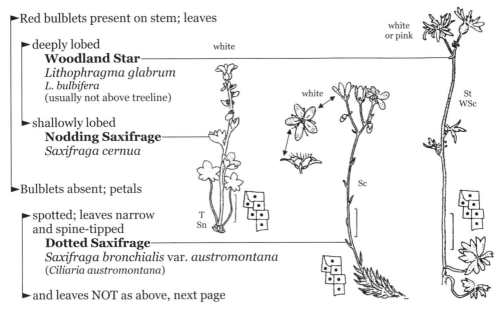

►Red bulblets present on stem; leaves

► deeply lobed
Woodland Star————————white
Lithophragma glabrum
L. bulbifera
(usually not above treeline)

white
or pink

white

St
WSc

► shallowly lobed
Nodding Saxifrage
Saxifraga cernua

Sc

►Bulblets absent; petals

► spotted; leaves narrow
and spine-tipped
Dotted Saxifrage————————
Saxifraga bronchialis var. *austromontana*
(*Ciliaria austromontana*)

T
Sn

► and leaves NOT as above, next page

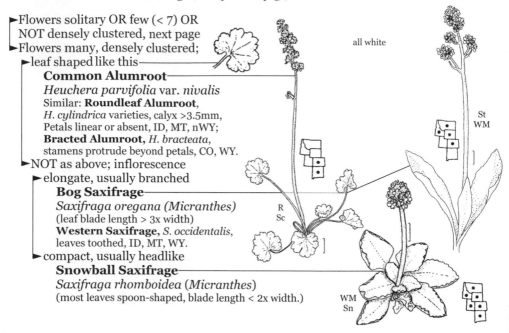

►Flowers solitary OR few (< 7) OR
NOT densely clustered, next page
►Flowers many, densely clustered;
  ►leaf shaped like this──────
    Common Alumroot──────
    Heuchera parvifolia var. *nivalis*
    Similar: **Roundleaf Alumroot**,
    H. cylindrica varieties, calyx >3.5mm,
    Petals linear or absent, ID, MT, nWY;
    Bracted Alumroot, *H. bracteata*,
    stamens protrude beyond petals, CO, WY.
►NOT as above; inflorescence
  ►elongate, usually branched
    Bog Saxifrage──────
    Saxifraga oregana (Micranthes)
    (leaf blade length > 3x width)
    Western Saxifrage, *S. occidentalis*,
    leaves toothed, ID, MT, WY.
  ►compact, usually headlike
    Snowball Saxifrage──────
    Saxifraga rhomboidea (Micranthes)
    (most leaves spoon-shaped, blade length < 2x width.)

all white

St
WM

R
Sc

WM
Sn

►Stem with more than one leaf, next page

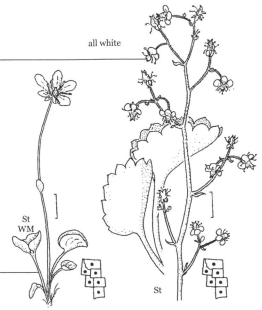

►Stem leafless; petals NOT fringed
Brook Saxifrage
Saxifraga odontoloma
(*S. arguta, Micranthes*)
(stems green, mostly > 30cm or 12in tall)

all white

Red-stemmed Saxifrage, *S. lyallii*,
usually < 20cm (8in) tall, ID, MT;

Tolmie's Saxifrage, *S. tolmiei*, very thick
and fleshy stonecrop-like leaves, ID, MT.

Kotzebue's Grass-of-Parnassus,
P. kotzebuei, uncommon,
inconspicuous, < 10cm (4in) tall,
CO, MT, WY.

►Stem with one leaf; petals fringed
Fringed Grass-of-Parnassus
Parnassia fimbriata

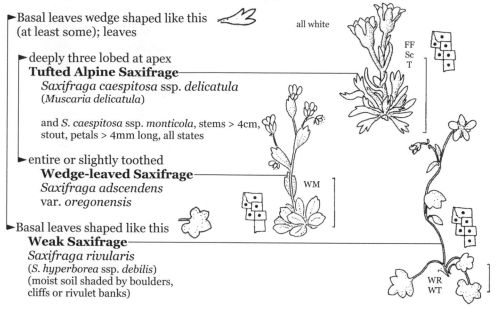

►Basal leaves wedge shaped like this (at least some); leaves

all white

► deeply three lobed at apex
Tufted Alpine Saxifrage
Saxifraga caespitosa ssp. *delicatula*
(*Muscaria delicatula*)

and *S. caespitosa* ssp. *monticola*, stems > 4cm, stout, petals > 4mm long, all states

► entire or slightly toothed
Wedge-leaved Saxifrage
Saxifraga adscendens
var. *oregonensis*

►Basal leaves shaped like this
Weak Saxifrage
Saxifraga rivularis
(*S. hyperborea* ssp. *debilis*)
(moist soil shaded by boulders, cliffs or rivulet banks)

FF
Sc
T

WM

WR
WT

FIGWORT FAMILY (*Scrophulariaceae*) Flowers irregular with four or five united petals or none AND with 2 or 4 fertile stamens, or 4 fertile plus 1 sterile stamen. Ovary superior. Fruit a shallowly 2-lobed capsule.

▶ Stem leaves opposite (at least lower leaves), page 122

▶ Stem leaves alternate OR entirely basal; stamens

　▶ NOT extending beyond petals, page 119

　▶ extend beyond petals (calyx if no petals); petals

　　▶ absent
　　　Wyoming Kittentails
　　　Besseya wyomingensis

　　▶ present, next page

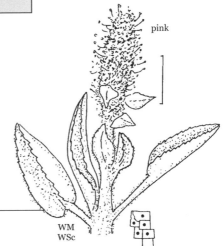

pink

WM
WSc

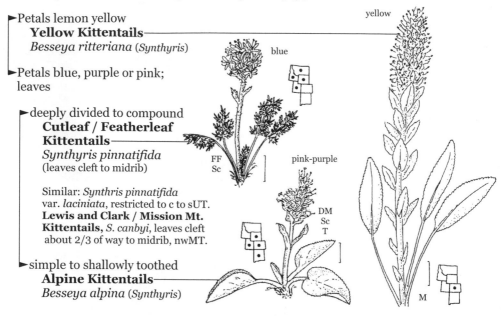

►Petals lemon yellow
  Yellow Kittentails
   Besseya ritteriana (*Synthyris*)

►Petals blue, purple or pink; leaves

  ►deeply divided to compound
    Cutleaf / Featherleaf Kittentails
     Synthyris pinnatifida (leaves cleft to midrib)

    Similar: *Synthris pinnatifida* var. *laciniata*, restricted to c to sUT.
    Lewis and Clark / Mission Mt. Kittentails, *S. canbyi*, leaves cleft about 2/3 of way to midrib, nwMT.

  ►simple to shallowly toothed
    Alpine Kittentails
     Besseya alpina (*Synthyris*)

yellow

blue

FF
Sc

pink-purple

DM
Sc
T

M

►Inflorescence looks like it was dipped
　in paint (Paintbrushes), and is
　　►greenish to yellow
　　　　Beautiful Paintbrush ──────
　　　　Castilleja pulchella
　　　　(glandular and long soft hairs)
　　　　Others: **Snow Paintbrush,** *C. nivea,*
　　　　shaggy hairs, MT, WY; **Western Yellow
　　　　Paintbrush,** *C. occidentalis,* leaves mostly entire,
　　　　usually above treeline, all states but MT; **Alpine
　　　　Paintbrush,** *C. puberula,* leaves very narrow or
　　　　narrowly lobed, CO; **Northern Paintbrush,**
　　　　C. sulphurea, plant hardly hairy, stem > 20cm (8in),
　　　　leaves entire, mostly below treeline, all states.
　　►red to magenta
　　　　Rosy Paintbrush ──────
　　　　Castilleja rhexifolia
　　　　(crosses with *C. sulphurea* and *C. miniata*
　　　　producing many color and leaf variations)
　　　　Others: **Beautiful Paintbrush,** *C. pulchella,* long soft
　　　　hairs, see above; **Hayden's Paintbrush,** *C. haydenii,*
　　　　bracts and leaves linear lobed, hot pink, sCO, NM.
►Inflorescence NOT as above, next page

yellowish
to purplish

pink
to red

WM
FF
T

M

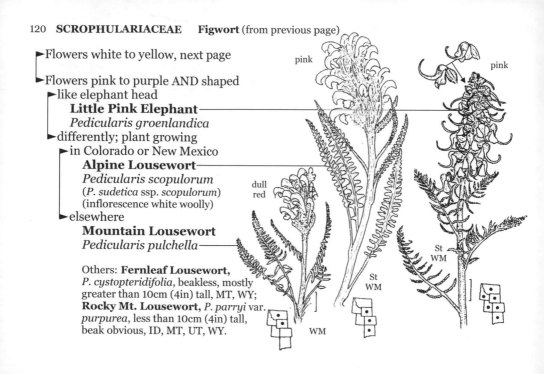

►Flowers white to yellow, next page

►Flowers pink to purple AND shaped
  ►like elephant head
    Little Pink Elephant
    Pedicularis groenlandica
  ►differently; plant growing
    ►in Colorado or New Mexico
      Alpine Lousewort
      Pedicularis scopulorum
      (*P. sudetica* ssp. *scopulorum*)
      (inflorescence white woolly)
    ►elsewhere
      Mountain Lousewort
      Pedicularis pulchella

Others: **Fernleaf Lousewort,**
P. cystopteridifolia, beakless, mostly
greater than 10cm (4in) tall, MT, WY;
Rocky Mt. Lousewort, *P. parryi* var.
purpurea, less than 10cm (4in) tall,
beak obvious, ID, MT, UT, WY.

pink

pink

dull
red

St
WM

St
WM

WM

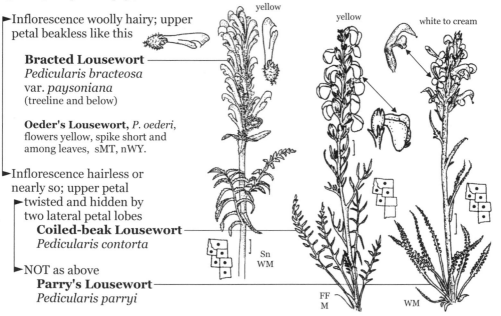

▶Inflorescence woolly hairy; upper petal beakless like this

Bracted Lousewort
Pedicularis bracteosa
var. *paysoniana*
(treeline and below)

Oeder's Lousewort, *P. oederi*,
flowers yellow, spike short and
among leaves, sMT, nWY.

▶Inflorescence hairless or
nearly so; upper petal
▶twisted and hidden by
two lateral petal lobes
Coiled-beak Lousewort
Pedicularis contorta

▶NOT as above
Parry's Lousewort
Pedicularis parryi

yellow

yellow

white to cream

Sn
WM

FF
M

WM

►Petals blue, purple, lavender, pink to dirty whitish
OR white with dark veins, next page

►Petals greenish white to cream OR pale pink
James' Snowlover
Chionophila jamesii
(flowers tightly bunched on short stem)

Tweedy's Snowlover, *C. tweedyi,* flowers
spaced on elongate stem, cID, swMT,
(drawing on page 124).

►Petals yellow
Alpine Monkeyflower
Mimulus tilingii
(creeping rhizomes, flowers 1 – 5
per stem, 2-4cm /0.8-1.6in long)

Yellow / Seep Monkeyflower,
M. guttatus, flowers smaller and
often > 5 per stem, mostly below
treeline, all states.

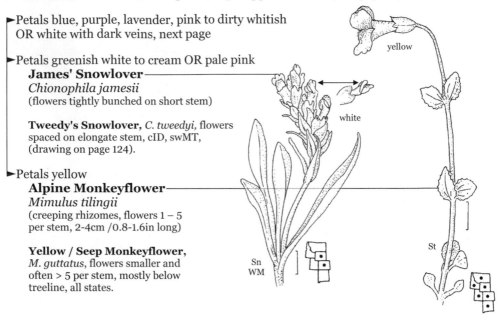

yellow

white

Sn
WM

St

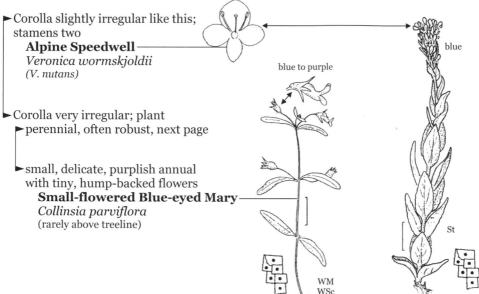

► Corolla slightly irregular like this;
stamens two
    Alpine Speedwell
    Veronica wormskjoldii
    (V. nutans)

blue

► Corolla very irregular; plant
 ► perennial, often robust, next page

blue to purple

► small, delicate, purplish annual
with tiny, hump-backed flowers
    Small-flowered Blue-eyed Mary
    Collinsia parviflora
    (rarely above treeline)

St

WM
WSc

▶Flowers large, over 1.5cm,
next page

▶Flowers smaller; inflorescence

▶one-sided
Tweedy's Snowlover
Chionophila tweedyi

▶head-like or in whorls
Littleflower Penstemon
Penstemon procerus
(*P. confertus* ssp. *procerus*)
(flowers less than 1cm long, nodding;
anther sacs almost round and opening flat)

Similar: **Rydberg's Penstemon,**
P. rydbergia, flowers > 1cm long,
usually ascending, anther sacs oval and
not spreading flat, all states.

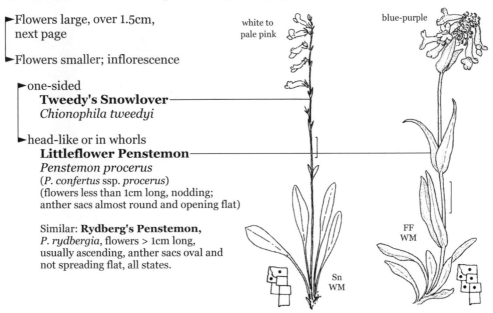

white to
pale pink

blue-purple

FF
WM

Sn
WM

Figwort (from previous page)

► Stems creeping or sprawling in unstable scree or talus, next page

► Stems NOT sprawling, mostly erect, herbaceous; leaves

   ► very narrow (< 5 mm wide), linear elongate or slightly widened and rounded at tip
     Hall's Penstemon
     Penstemon hallii
     (forms mats)

   ► wider; corolla with obvious glandular hairs
     Dusky Penstemon
     Penstemon whippleanus

► Stems bushy AND woody at least below, next page

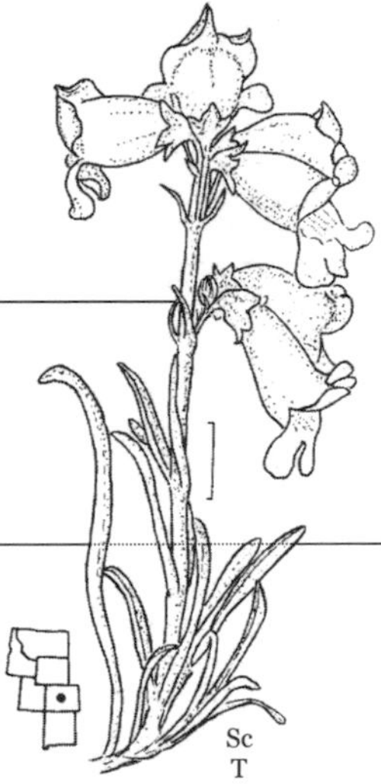

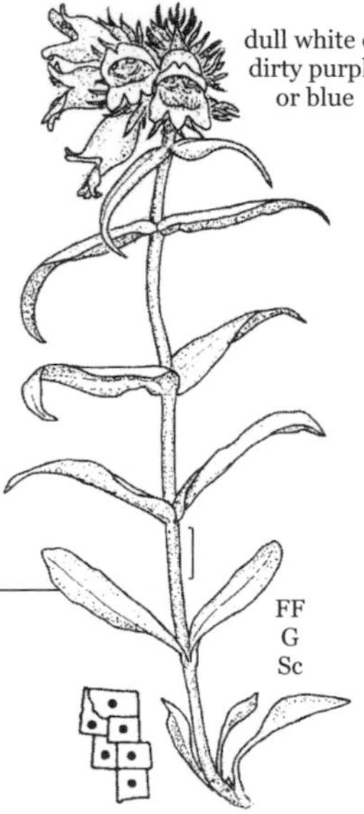

blue to magenta

dull white or dirty purple or blue

Sc
T

FF
G
Sc

blue to
lavender-purple

►Stems woody, tending to sprawl
Shrubby Penstemon—
Penstemon fruticosus
(mostly below treeline)

lavender-purple

►Stems creeping or sprawling, NOT woody
►leaves toothed,
anthers densely hairy—
Mountain Penstemon—
Penstemon montanus

USc
R

Rockvine Penstemon, *P. ellipticus*,
sterile stamen densely hairy, ID, MT.

blue to purple

G
R

►leaves entire, anthers not hairy
Harbour's Penstemon—
Penstemon harbourii

FF
USc

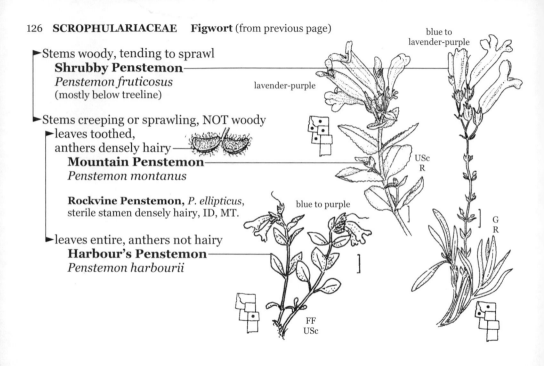

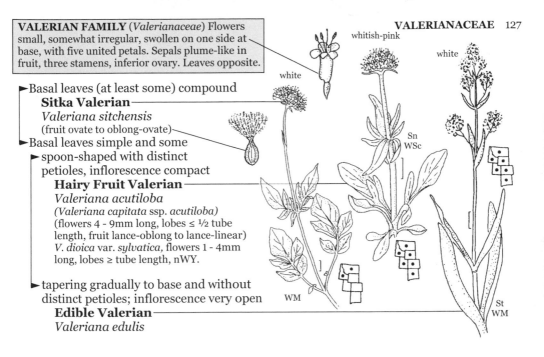

VALERIAN FAMILY (*Valerianaceae*) Flowers small, somewhat irregular, swollen on one side at base, with five united petals. Sepals plume-like in fruit, three stamens, inferior ovary. Leaves opposite.

whitish-pink

white

white

white

►Basal leaves (at least some) compound
  Sitka Valerian
  Valeriana sitchensis
  (fruit ovate to oblong-ovate)
►Basal leaves simple and some
  ► spoon-shaped with distinct
    petioles, inflorescence compact
    Hairy Fruit Valerian
    Valeriana acutiloba
    (*Valeriana capitata* ssp. *acutiloba*)
    (flowers 4 - 9mm long, lobes ≤ ½ tube
    length, fruit lance-oblong to lance-linear)
    V. dioica var. *sylvatica*, flowers 1 - 4mm
    long, lobes ≥ tube length, nWY.

  ► tapering gradually to base and without
    distinct petioles; inflorescence very open
    Edible Valerian
    Valeriana edulis

Sn
WSc

WM

St
WM

VIOLET FAMILY (*Violaceae*)
Flowers irregular with five separate petals.
Leaves usually simple, alternate or basal.

Mountain Blue Violet
Viola labradorica
(*V. adunca*)

Two-flowered Violet, *V. biflora,*
flowers yellow, CO.

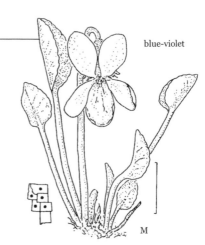

blue-violet

M

Janet L. Wingate, M.S., Ph.D., a botanist and taxonomist, is Herbarium Manager of the Kathryn Kalmbach Herbarium at the Denver Botanic Gardens. Dr. Wingate is the author and illustrator of many botanical articles and books including *Rocky Mountain Flower Finder* and *Illustrated Keys to the Grasses of Colorado.*

Loraine Yeatts is a field botanist and taxonomist specializing in alpine and desert floras, and an accomplished wildflower photographer and international lecturer. She has conducted several botanical surveys including one for the National Park Service of Rocky Mountain National Park (1987 to 1992) with the assistance of Janet Wingate, and others from the Denver Botanic Gardens, Kathryn Kalmbach Herbarium.

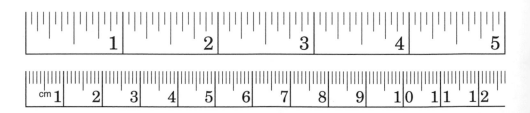